12-29-70

White-Collar Blacks

White-Collar Blacks

A Breakthrough?

John S. Morgan
Richard L. Van Dyke

American Management Association, Inc.

Photo Credits

*p. 46—Hopkins Photography; p. 48—Matar Studio; p. 88
—Madison Geddes; p. 115—Robert Houston; p. 119—
Stephen Stegel; p. 153—Wagner International Photos,
Inc.; p. 184—Pach Bros.; p. 190—Martin Schweig.*

International standard book number 0-8144-5235-3
Library of Congress catalog card number: 74-119385

First printing

1574103

To the forty-four men and women
who cooperated in making this book possible

Contents

PART ONE

Introduction

WHITE-COLLAR BLACKS:
IS THERE A
BREAKTHROUGH?

The current efforts to employ more members of the so-called "hard-core" unemployed groups, especially Negroes, are bearing fruit. Organizations like the National Alliance of Businessmen are experiencing measurable success. But still an ironic fact remains: Employment of better-educated, more advantaged blacks in business and industry is increasing at only a snail's pace. The better the education and environmental background of Negroes, the less relative improvement they apparently are achieving in gaining a foothold in the business establishment.

In a report on 4,249 New York City businesses, for example, the federal Equal Employment Opportunity Commission found that 43 percent had no Negro white-collar employees in 1967. The same agency surveyed 100 major companies based in New York, companies that contribute nearly 16 percent of our gross national product. The study showed that in 1966, blacks made up only 2.6 percent of the headquarters staffs of these companies; this figure is to be compared with the citywide average of 5.2 percent in white-collar job categories. The commission obtained the 1967 figures for 70 of these corporations before releasing the report: these figures showed that the number of Negro white-collar workers had increased only very slightly, from 2.5 percent in 1966 to 3.2 percent in 1967. Although comparable data are not available for white-collar employment in other cities, it is very probable that business and industry do worse outside New York City so far as the employment of Negroes in such positions is concerned.

A mid-1969 survey of the 441 companies enrolled in the government-industry Plans for Progress program, a voluntary effort to employ more minority-group members in industry, showed that of the more than 1.8 million officials, managers, and professionals employed by these firms, only 18,779, or about 1 percent, were black. And of this number, only a relative handful could accurately be described as executives.

So concerned are Negroes themselves about the situation that they have formed the Council of Concerned Black Executives, Inc., an organization based in New York, "to work towards the inclusion of black men and women in the full spectrum of American corporate life."

Why Bother?

Some white managers and professional men may view with indifference or even private satisfaction the fact that relatively few blacks are in their ranks. And some Negroes regard with cynicism the current efforts by business and industry to increase recruiting in white-collar job areas. They attribute these efforts to corporate leaders' fear that the nation faces a social upheaval unless full racial integration occurs at all levels of employment. Negroes contend that the black-power movement and the riots and other racial disturbances of recent years have created a new awareness that "showcase" hiring of a few blacks, often at low levels of responsibility, isn't enough.

Such pressures have probably played their part in making corporations concerned about integration at the white-collar level, but other factors may be still more influential—for example:

Labor-market pressures. The current shortage of manpower extends all the way from skilled crafts through top management. Today there aren't enough young, college-educated adults coming into business—the type of people who fill almost all the managerial and professional positions in industry. Of the more than 20 million people aged 18 through 25 in the United States today, only 11 percent have graduated or eventually will graduate from college. This is not enough to meet the burgeoning demand for managers and professionals. As a result, corporate personnel men cannot afford to overlook anybody, including the growing numbers of college-educated blacks.

Government expectations. On July 4, 1776, the Continental Congress signed the Declaration of Independence, in which it declared that all men are created equal. On January 1, 1863, President Lincoln issued his Emancipation Proclamation. On June 25, 1941,

President Roosevelt issued an Executive Order stating, "It is the policy of the United States to encourage full participation in the national defense program by all citizens of the United States, regardless of race, creed, color, or national origin. . . ." The current law covering employment integration is Title VII of the Civil Rights Act of 1964, which is administered by the Equal Employment Opportunity Commission. Most employers who contract with the federal government are covered by Executive Order 11246, relating to equal employment, which is administered by the Labor Department's Office of Federal Contract Compliance.

The federal government, then, requires job integration—as do many state and local governments. The government cannot have expected much job integration when the Declaration of Independence was signed—but it does today, as many employers have discovered.

Social pressures. Public expectations in this area are also significant, and this creates more pressure on companies. Public-opinion polls show that the most urgent domestic problem, as seen by the general public, is race relations; and many closely related issues also rank high—riots, civil disturbance, breakdown of law and order. Sixty percent of the public believe that companies should take an active role in combating social ills, including racial discrimination. A very high proportion—83 percent—believe that companies should do more than they are doing now.

Corporate conscience. Ralph Lazarus, chairman of Federated Department Stores, Inc., echoes the thoughts of many businessmen when he says: "The great challenge to leadership in our age is the challenge of violence—the violence that follows a head-on collision between the forces of change and inflexible, dehumanized organizations in too many areas of American life, including business. This violence is weakening our institutions. It is opening the doors to repression and shifting the odds that freedom can survive the conflicts and complexities of tomorrow.

"If the corporation wants to help swing the odds back toward freedom, it must meet the forces of change with new forms of openness and flexibility based on the needs of its own individuals. As one of the largest of our human organizations, it can defuse the causes of violence more effectively through its people than through its economic power. It can help restructure society by first restructuring itself. . . .

"History tells us that the societies with the greatest thrust have been those that encourage self-respect by recognizing diversity and providing the individual a chance to play an active role."

Thus conscience plays its role, too, in leading to more integration.

Why Not More White-Collar Blacks?

Answers to this question may sound like these:

- "We want to hire qualified blacks, but there aren't enough— for those there are, the competition is tremendous."
- "Only five Negro colleges graduate engineers, and only two of these programs are accredited."
- "Show us some qualified people, and we'll hire them this afternoon."

Such arguments, unfortunately, hold some truth, but the problem goes even deeper. For example, listen to the experiences of a white recruiter who specializes in finding black people for managerial and professional jobs in a large company. He interviewed seven successful blacks already with the organization, seeking their advice on how to do a better job. Here are his personal, subjective impressions:

"The blacks have guilty consciences about having 'made it' in a white business. They have acted as 'white' as they could and are uneasy about having succeeded under false colors.

"They tend to see things in a different context than whites, even though they have had years of experience in white management circles. Examples: They take things literally and take the company's word as gospel. If the organization doesn't do things exactly as it says it will, they feel the company has lost credibility. This applies in the area of prediction, particularly. If we say we're going to be making money on a new product by the first half of the year, but don't, they take this as an outrage. A white, by contrast, would expect the slippage and not be nearly as upset.

"On the other hand, blacks think whites have a hang-up about getting to work on time, meeting deadlines, doing everything on a timetable. In their culture, deadlines are not as important as they are for whites. Blacks can't understand the fuss.

14

"They also read into things meanings that a white never would. They are supersensitive about race. They do not really want integration, but they recognize that separatism (which they really want) is not practical socially or economically. They have their own filters of perception. This accounts, perhaps, for the fact that they don't seem to perceive what's going on in the company in the same way whites do. They don't perceive the needs of a manager in the same way. From a white's viewpoint, they don't quite know what's going on. It's as though they were reading a newspaper through a filter of water."

A harsh judgment? But remember that it comes from a man who, although white, has been charged with the responsibility of hiring more blacks for white-collar jobs and helping them become successful. Is he critical because he's trying to understand what his problems are? Aside from the most obvious problem—shortage of qualified people and, as a result, excessive competition by employers for the limited number available—he sees three major hurdles to be overcome if more complete integration of the white-collar ranks is to be achieved.

1. *The difference between black culture and white culture.* "This has more importance in the office than in the factory environment," says the recruiter. "In most hourly jobs, a man must conform to quite clearly set rules and standards, usually dictated by the machine or the product. But in the office the atmosphere is more fluid, less mechanistic. Human qualities count for more; therefore, the cultural differences have more importance. The different attitudes toward time become more noticeable, for example. In the factory, you conform in this area or get out. Not necessarily so in the office. Different cultural attitudes show up in off-job interests, too—in dress, in educational emphasis, in attitudes toward the family." The recruiter emphasizes that he is not critical of the differences; he is merely pointing out that more accommodation must be made for cultural diversities in business and industry.

2. *The minority syndrome and defensive psychology.* "Psychologists might be able to explain this better than I can," says the recruiter. "The Negroes I have observed in white-collar jobs tend to be cliquey, somewhat insular, slow to mix with whites. This has been noticeable even after some strenuous efforts by whites to make them welcome. I know that this results from generations of ostracism by white society. I know it can't be changed overnight. But I also know that it causes problems. With some exceptions, blacks tend to two extremes in the

office—too much conformity or too much aggression. Neither helps the operation much."

3. *Different perceptions.* The recruiter points out that the differences in cultures and this defensive psychology contribute significantly to differences in perceptions of facts and opinions. "For example," he says, "many blacks don't believe that white managers truly want them in their ranks. Some don't think that I really want them even though I spend all my working time in recruiting them. They think my boss has given me this job and I'm only performing like a good soldier. Such perceptions depress me because I honestly believe that most whites do not now object to blacks in white-collar jobs. However, there are white managers who still show prejudice. Negroes have been conspicuously absent from managerial ranks in most white-dominated companies for centuries. A black's cynical perceptions about the current white attitudes toward him in the office are understandable if regrettable."

But the recruiter adds that varying perceptions are sometimes beneficial. He comments: "I always remember the example of a new product sales promotion campaign. We have a gifted Negro in sales promotion who was uncharacteristically lukewarm about an ad program. He said it might be offensive, not to blacks but to whites. The theme had some good-natured fun and play on words concerning integration and the generation gap. He was probably more perceptive than his white colleagues to the psychological implications. I think we were fortunate to have his different viewpoint. In any event, we took his advice and chose a different theme. And, incidentally, I owe my job to the perceptions of some of the Negro managers in my own company. A black was first considered for the position, but they vetoed him because he was a 'white' Negro and would not be accepted by some of his own race. I had been doing some work in race relations for the company that had received considerable publicity in the black press, and the Negro managers recommended me."

Basis for Optimism?

Despite the generally lackluster record for job integration in white-collar work, there is some basis for optimism about the future.

For example, a Labor Department analysis in early 1969 reported

16

a "sharp acceleration" in the movement of black workers into "higher status" jobs. About two-thirds of the net increase in Negro employment from 1962 to 1967 was in professional, technical, managerial, clerical, and sales positions. Black employment in those years fell by 600,000 in the less attractive categories—domestic service, industrial labor, and farm work—the study showed.

Some significant statistics in the five-year upgrading: Salaried managerial jobs held by black people went up 49 percent, to 115,000; teaching positions rose 46 percent, to 202,000; clerical jobs went up 76 percent, to 890,000. Negroes made sizable gains in better-paying manufacturing jobs, police and fire department work, and medical and other health work.

Although nearly half of all employed Negroes held unskilled, service, or farm jobs, compared with only one-fifth of all white workers, there has been a relative improvement in job satisfaction among blacks, which would indicate that they are aware of their gains. A mid-1969 Gallup poll found that 76 percent of the Negroes queried were satisfied with their jobs, compared with only 55 percent who were satisfied in 1949. However, 88 percent of the whites were satisfied in 1969, as compared with 69 percent in 1949.

The educational situation also offers some grounds for optimism, both because more black people are going to college and because more "white establishment" companies now recruit in the predominantly black colleges which about 40 percent of all Negro undergraduates attend.

The scramble for Negro college graduates has intensified over the past few years. Black students at Columbia's business school got more job offers than whites in 1969 at salaries "5 to 10 percent higher" than the whites received, a university official reported. The number of corporate recruiters visiting five Negro colleges in the Atlanta area in 1969 was up 25 percent from a year earlier.

Business schools recruit more Negro students. At Harvard's Graduate School of Business, a special recruiting drive boosted the number of black students to 105 in the 1969–1970 school year from about 30 the previous year. The University of Pennsylvania's Wharton School increased its Negro enrollment up to 32 from only 4 in 1966–1967 by sending recruiters to predominantly black colleges for the first time. Expanded junior-college recruiting helped UCLA double the number of blacks in its graduate business school since 1968–1969. Yet, less than 2.5 percent of the students in 15 major graduate business schools are from minority groups, according to a recent survey by the Alfred P. Sloan Foundation. The foundation has given a newly created council of nine schools a $1 million grant to provide more fellowships and counseling for minority students. Harvard assigns a faculty member to raise fellowship funds for black students.

Still, a Negro executive recruiter figures that it will take 15 years before blacks hold corporate vice-presidencies in significant numbers, because it will take some years before enough Negroes with an interest in business graduate from college. Although Negroes constitute about 12.5 percent of the college-age population, they account for only about 6.5 percent of all high school graduates, according to figures compiled by the U.S. Office of Education. And probably only about half of all black high school graduates are fully capable of handling a college curriculum, according to an estimate by Fred E. Crossland, an education expert with the Ford Foundation. "Given present standards," Mr. Crossland says, "it's preposterous and statistically impossible to talk about boosting black enrollment to 10 percent even over the next five years."

Despite the statistical anomalies, proportionately more Negro graduates are going into business at the expense of the traditional "teaching and preaching" professions. Take the case of Morehouse College in Atlanta, a 1,000-student liberal arts institution whose most famous alumnus is the Reverend Dr. Martin Luther King, Jr. (class of 1948). Until recently, the large majority of Morehouse graduates went into the traditional fields. But, of the 1969 class of 131, only 3 entered the ministry, 6 went into education, and 15 entered law school. Sixty percent of the class went on to graduate school or entered different professional fields. One graduate, in fact, turned down 22 job offers to continue on at a graduate business school.

Of course, this last fact points up the continuing scarcity of qualified Negro graduates. Although more Negroes now go to college, they generally constitute a tiny minority in the predominantly white colleges where most companies recruit. Black enrollment in 37 major "white" schools at the start of the 1969–1970 school year was only 3.6 percent of the total number of undergraduates. However, this percentage will rise: in these schools, the proportion of blacks in the freshman class was generally much higher than 3.6 percent.

THE METHOD OF THIS BOOK

Both black and white managers and professionals are troubled by the following key questions concerning ways and means to get more Negroes into their ranks:

1. How can more black people be recruited?
2. How can they be better trained, once they have been recruited?
3. How can they be more fairly promoted, once they have been trained?
4. How can employers improve the odds that good black employees will stay with them?
5. How can employers improve their communication with black employees?

One way to answer such questions is to find out what blacks think who have "made it" in managerial or professional capacities in the predominantly white business establishment. We have done this in interviews with 44 such Negroes. Their answers to these questions, which have been incorporated in their biographies, constitute the frame of reference of this book. Most of the interviewees commented on more than one question, and we have grouped the interviews according to their emphasis on each of the five principal areas of concern. Following the biographical interviews, there is a summary in which we have tried to present a consensus based on the interviews and to present conclusions from other sources as well.

Some readers may doubt that blacks in significant numbers can handle white-collar jobs. But, to a man (or woman), all the Negroes we have interviewed say they can. And nearly all whites who have had experience dealing with blacks in white-collar work agree with this opinion.

But this is just one important opinion. A statistical summary of the responses of the managers and professionals interviewed reveals some other strong views about the role of white-collar blacks in business. In the following pages, we present an overview of their replies.

HOW THE RESPONDENTS
ANSWERED

We have highlighted the salient points that emerged in our interviews to draw attention to common threads appearing in the biographies. Answers were sought to questions such as the following: Are there many Negroes qualified *now* for managerial positions? Where do you find them? How do you recruit them? What characteristics seem essential to the Negro manager or professional? Do such characteristics differ from those essential to whites? What special problems do Negro managers and professionals have in business? How can present managers—white or black—help solve them? What is the attitude of the white worker toward black coworkers? What areas of business or regions of the country would be most hospitable to the ambitious black man or woman?

Here is a sampling of areas in which the respondents call for reforms: promotion practices, identification of potential, attitudes of white coworkers, salary differential, recruitment, treatment on the job, and living and working conditions.

Higher Job Qualifications

Eighty-five percent of the respondents answered yes to the question: "Do you believe there are numerous minority-group members now qualified for managerial or professional positions who do not hold them?" One interviewee summed up the situation by saying, "A significant number of minority personnel have been 'passed over,' especially those individuals in the age range of 40 to 55 years. Those in that age group have had to face considerable discrimination while they were in their prime." However, others felt that the number of qualified people available is small, since relatively few blacks are in management training programs.

This indicates a feeling that there is a lack of upward mobility; moreover, a sizable number of the interviewees (65 percent) felt that industry requires blacks to excel and be superior to whites to maintain their positions. One actual case is a good example: A black employee had assignments with four divisions of a large corporation, and his budget for all the projects for the four divisions equaled the budget of a white coworker—with less experience and training than the Negro—who worked on only one major account. The black had to report to and work with some 20 people in a diversity of situations, while his white coworker could concentrate on developing a program for only one product, with money to hire outside help and pay for all sorts of services.

Such superior qualifications have been required of Negroes over the years. To succeed at all, one had to be a "super Negro." The predominate feeling running through many of the interviews is the Negro's belief that whites categorize blacks in only two ways—either "superqualified" or substandard; there is, they believe, little tolerance of average talent among blacks.

Promotional Opportunities

Upward mobility was a major concern of 90 percent of those queried. This concern is understandable, considering what frugal use has been made of black talent in managerial positions in industry. One respondent sums it up: "Whether a social conscience or a need for government contracts spurs business to hire, the lack of promotional opportunities not only effectively stifles the working black but prevents others from moving into their entry-level slots."

When questioned about the problems facing blacks, but not most whites, in the white-collar ranks, 40 percent of the blacks cited "lack of promotional opportunities," and another 40 percent mentioned "prejudice." The rest indicated normal business inconsistencies.

How can present managers better identify the black potential manager or professional? The answer is, by constant communication and honest job evaluation: This response occurred 73 percent of the time.

The characteristics that 89 percent of those interviewed seem to consider essential to the black manager or professional are in the areas of communication, skill in performing assignments, and aggressiveness in pursuing increasing responsibilities. Do these characteristics differ from those needed by white managers and professionals? Sixty-three percent said no. But, interestingly enough, 37 percent answered yes, stating that the black employee must possess an abundance of talent in order to move ahead, more than is needed by white managers.

White managers can help blacks achieve promotions by encouraging and developing blacks through training programs and by allowing the employee to exercise greater responsibility, say 80 percent of the interviewees.

Attitudes

In general, how would you characterize the attitude of your white colleagues toward you? Of those interviewed, 60 percent felt that this attitude was condescending or superior, while 30 percent thought it was helpful and friendly. Only 10 percent answered, "About the same as toward other whites." Another attitude often mentioned was "discounting"—that is, a conscious or subconscious minimizing of a person's qualifications because he is black.

The advice most often given for present white managers who want to develop better relationships with black colleagues is—to repeat—communication (see Part Six). It is felt that true communication is essential and would assist blacks and whites to "get to know each other"; but, more important, it would set the stage for mutual respect.

Seventy-six percent of the men and women interviewed stated that the black employee is very often required to act as *the* Negro. "One is constantly called on to interpret the actions of all Negroes— from the janitor to the secretary to Whitney Young to Rap Brown." As a well-known star said in a radio interview, "No, it is not exciting to be constantly asked how it feels to be a star though black. It's a bore. I do it for my little sister and for all the other little sisters who may need to be encouraged."

Earning Power

To determine whether the relationship between salary and job responsibilities differs for black professionals and managers, the authors asked: "If you were white, how much more (as a percentage) do you estimate you would be earning now as compared with your present income?" Seventy-seven percent indicated that they would be earning more if they were white, and their estimates were as follows:

- 23 percent said they would earn 10 to 15 percent more.
- 39 percent said they would earn 15 to 20 percent more.
- 15 percent said they would earn 20 to 30 percent more.

Of the rest, 20.7 percent thought that their salaries would be about the same; and, surprisingly, 2.3 percent thought they would earn less if they were white.

Similarly, in estimating how their jobs would compare with those they would hold if they were white, 50 percent said their jobs would be better, 37 percent said their jobs would be the same, and 13 percent thought their jobs would be worse. Seven out of ten respondents said they were able to find housing commensurate with their employment status; this is unusual, considering the housing patterns around the country.

Recruitment

How can white managers help bring more Negroes into positions as managers, professionals, technicians, sales personnel, and office and clerical workers? "Stop talking about wanting to hire 'qualified' blacks, and act [hire]," demanded 63 percent of those interviewed. The rest gave such responses as these:

- "Do not use a white image for hiring blacks."
- "Review present black employees."
- "Make a management commitment, or goal, to hire a number of blacks based on the population makeup of the locality."
- "Recruit in black high schools, black colleges, and the black community" (see Part Two).

Applying these methods will help you find those talented employees.

In recruiting blacks, respondents believe, there are two types of potential employees: the "qualified" and the "qualifiable." The qualified black is easy to see, because he has more than enough education, experience, and *savoir faire* to do the job. The qualifiable individual may not have the education and experience normally required, but nevertheless he has the drive and potential to handle the assignment for which he is to be trained.

Can Negroes presently employed help bring more black people into white-collar jobs? Yes, was the overwhelming response. New job openings can be announced in the black communities through their newspapers and radio stations, high school career days, community organizations, black employment agencies, and the like. Managerial, professional, technical, and sales positions usually require a college education, but industry must review its demands as far as educational requirements are concerned, and perhaps look instead for performance on the job. Although the number of Negroes receiving degrees will increase significantly over the next five years (see accompanying table), the demand for talent will go even higher and can be alleviated only if industries modify their requirements and emphasize only those qualifications that are essential to job performance.

STATUS OF HIGHER EDUCATION AMONG BLACKS

Year	Total Students Earning Degrees	Percent of Total Who Are Black	No. of Blacks Earning Degrees	No. of Blacks Earning Technical Degrees	No. of Blacks Earning Nontechnical Degrees
1970	746,000	3.5	26,110	3,133	22,977
1971	760,000	4.0	34,200	4,104	30,096
1972	785,000	4.5	39,250	4,709	34,540
1973	821,000	5.0	45,155	5,417	39,736
1974	860,000	5.5	51,600	6,192	45,408
1975	898,000	6.0	58,370	7,003	51,365
1976	931,000	6.5	65,170	7,819	57,349
Total	5,801,000	5.2	319,855	38,377	281,471
Total percent of black graduates earning . . .				12	88

Source: Industry projections.

Special Treatment on the Job?

"Do you think that present managers should treat Negro white-collar employees differently from other white-collar employees?" Eighty percent of those questioned responded negatively to the idea of special treatment. They all wanted to be hired, promoted, and paid on the same basis as others. However, some agreed that there is a need for special training, and this opinion has some merit. A company must make a concentrated effort to bring Negroes into the economic mainstream. To do this requires an active recruitment program, realistic selection procedures, and a sensible training program —all of which means that special attention is needed to solve the problem.

Forty percent of those queried stated that if more Negroes are hired and exposed to the office environment, they can bring this information back into their families and communities, with the result that there is better counseling for new entrants into industry. The only logical answer to the question "How can Negroes be better motivated to perform in white-collar jobs?" is to have working conditions that show the Negro he can be promoted on the basis of his performance.

"Do you find it more difficult to manage or deal with white associates in your company than with members of your own race?" No, report six out of eight of the respondents. Those who answered yes said, "One way white managers can help blacks is to work to free themselves of attitudes which prevent promotions." This could be done by company programs, seminars, programs on human relations, and open discussions between blacks and whites. Many companies have sought to instill "black awareness" in white managers by requesting attendance at these types of sessions; these, however, are concentrating not on changing attitudes but on affecting *behavior* on the job.

Living and Working Conditions

Eighty-six percent of those asked said they would definitely advise their young children to try for managerial or professional careers in business and industry. The areas of employment suggested were the "nontraditional" Negro jobs—that is, careers that had been once considered "for whites only." The industries recommended for young black men and women coming out of college were banking, communications, manufacturing, and data processing. Data processing was mentioned most often. The professions recommended, in order of frequency, were technology (engineering, designing, and so on), business management (business administration, corporate law), sales, politics, finance, industrial relations, manufacturing, planning, and personnel administration.

When questioned as to whether problems for blacks vary according to the kind of business they work in (defense versus nondefense, for example) or the region in which they live, the yesses lost out five to three in favor of the noes. But both sides agreed that "nondefense" or private industry offered the best opportunities for advancement. The South led the parade in terms of presenting problems to blacks, but the North, East, and West were close seconds. Similarly, on the basis of what they had experienced or heard, 50 percent of the respondents said *no* area of the nation seemed more hospitable than any other for the ambitious black man or woman. However, the Northeast and the West Coast received some votes of confidence, along with Atlanta and Dallas.

In light of the advice that is reportedly given to young black sons and daughters, the young applicants who will soon be reaching business will be college-educated, determined to use their full talents and abilities, not afraid to try new ideas, and not tempted to sell their "blackness" for a position in public relations or urban affairs.

The black people interviewed showed a strong awareness that they are following in the footsteps of Negroes who have already performed effectively in managerial and professional capacities—almost since America was colonized. Let's examine the careers of a few of these men and women.

THE BLACK PROLOGUE

Before we review the experiences of Negroes who currently serve as white-collar employees in business and industry, let's look at the careers of a few remarkable blacks who blazed the way for their race in America years ago. From these we shall see that the goal of the Negro throughout the years has been integration into the mainstream of America.

Benjamin Banneker
(1731–1806)

Benjamin Banneker was born and educated in Maryland. While still a youth, he made a wooden clock which ran accurately for the rest of his life. From 1791 until 1802 Banneker published a yearly almanac. He was the first of his race to publish scientific and astronomical materials in the United States. He also published a treatise on bees and computed the cycle of the 17-year locust. He studied the stars at night and slept during the day. When he was not sleeping, he worked on mathematical computations.

Banneker also contributed to the field of engineering. He was a member of the surveying team which laid out the city plan for the nation's capital.

Oscar James Dunn
(1826–1871)

Oscar James Dunn, who was a lieutenant governor of Louisiana, was born a slave in New Orleans. At the age of 15, he ran away from his cruel master; later, he purchased his freedom. He was sufficiently skilled as a plasterer and house painter to earn a comfortable living. When federal troops occupied Louisiana at the close of the Civil War, Dunn worked for the Freedmen's Bureau as a traveling agent, checking the employment policies of plantation owners who were hiring Negro laborers.

Before his service with the Freedmen's Bureau, Dunn had opened an employment service in New Orleans to guide former slave laborers in their role as free laborers. His services involved drawing up contracts and interpreting the conditions of work and the wages to be received by Negroes. At the same time, he opened a bakery which employed a large number of free laborers.

In 1868, Dunn was elected lieutenant governor on the Republican ticket. Presiding over the senate with courage and firmness, he was regarded as incorruptible, even by the Democrats. He placed honesty above personal gain and was outspoken in his distaste for graft and corruption in office.

Henry Ossian Flipper
(1856–1940)

Henry Ossian Flipper, the first Negro to graduate from the U.S. Military Academy at West Point, was born in Thomasville, Georgia. After the liberation of the slaves in 1865, the Flipper family moved to Atlanta, where Henry was educated at a school conducted by the American Missionary Association and at Atlanta University. He won his appointment to West Point while he was studying at Atlanta University. His graduation from the Military Academy in 1877 attracted the attention of the nation's leading newspapers. The New York *Herald* said that Cadet Flipper was the only one to receive cheers at the graduation exercises.

As early as 1877, there was some concern about Second Lieutenant Flipper's request for cavalry service because there were reports of an army regulation which prohibited black officers in white regiments. In 1878, because of this controversy, he was assigned to the 10th Cavalry at Fort Sill, one of two colored regular-army cavalry regiments authorized by Congress in 1866.

After leaving the army, Flipper became an engineer; on his retirement in 1930, he was recognized as an outstanding petroleum engineer.

Lloyd Augustus Hall
(1894–   )

Lloyd Augustus Hall, as chief chemist and director of research for Griffith Laboratories of Chicago, revolutionized the meat-packing industry with his discoveries of curing salts for the preserving and processing of meats. He has more than 25 patents registered in the U.S. Patent Office for processes used in the manufacturing and packaging of food products, especially meats and bakery products.

During World War I Hall was assistant chief inspector of high explosives with the ordnance department of the U.S. Army. His success in this field came through concentrated training in the sciences. He was an honor graduate in science from East High School of Aurora, Illinois, earned the degrees of bachelor of science and pharmaceutical chemist from Northwestern University, and followed his training with special graduate work at the University of Chicago and the University of Illinois.

Percy L. Julian
(1898–   )

Dr. Percy L. Julian, millionaire scientist, businessman, and former teacher, graduated from DePauw University in 1920 as valedictorian of his class and Phi Beta Kappa orator. He taught at Fisk, West Virginia State, Howard, and DePauw universities. Dr. Julian was born in Montgomery, Alabama, where his father was a railroad clerk. Julian's gifted mind earned him scholarships to Harvard and the University of Vienna. During his college years at DePauw, he slept in the attic of a fraternity house where he worked as a waiter to earn his room and board.

After leaving the academic world, Dr. Julian became director of research for the Glidden Corporation in Chicago. He later established his own company, Julian Laboratories, where he developed soybean products, hormone preparations, and other pharmaceuticals. Dr. Julian is credited with having made the drug Cortisone available to consumers at a reasonable cost.

Thomy Lafon
(1810–1893)

Thomy Lafon, philanthropist, was born in New Orleans. After an education that qualified him to be a schoolteacher, he became a merchant and invested his money in real estate. Lafon learned the thrifty habit of saving and investing early in life, and he became one of the richest men in New Orleans. Having experienced the sting of poverty as a young boy, Lafon spent the remainder of his life helping the needy regardless of their race, creed, or color. At his death he left an estate valued at $600,000 to charity. Because he had considerable wealth, the city of New Orleans on one occasion borrowed money from him.

William Alexander Leidesdorff
(1810–1848)

William Alexander Leidesdorff was born on St. Croix in the U.S. Virgin Islands. He and his brother were sent to New Orleans to work in their father's cotton business. When his brother died, Leidesdorff took the capital he inherited and in 1841 sailed on a schooner for California, where he played an exciting and influential role in the political struggle between Mexico and the United States for possession of California.

Leidesdorff bought land in San Francisco and in 1844 obtained a tract of 35,000 acres on the American River from the government. In 1846 he became the American consul in California and city treasurer of San Francisco. Not only a politician but also a sportsman, he introduced horse racing to California. When he died at the age of only 38, he left an estate that was valued at $1,500,000. His great wealth came primarily from the land he owned on the American River, which was one of the sites of the famous gold strike in 1849.

Jan Ernst Matzeliger
(1852–1889)

Jan Ernst Matzeliger was born in Dutch Guiana. At the age of ten he started to work in a machine shop. Although he could speak little English, young Jan earned his passage to the United States as a sailor. He found work in Philadelphia and later moved to Lynn, Massachusetts, where he learned shoemaking, a trade in which he worked for the remainder of his life.

Before he died, he had invented the lasting machine, which revolutionized the manufacture of shoes and helped make Lynn the shoe capital of the world. Mechanization of shoemaking had been applied to the cutting and stitching of leather, but the final problem of shaping and attaching the upper portion of the shoe to the leather sole still remained. Matzeliger worked for ten years perfecting the "lasting machine" and on March 20, 1883, received his U.S. patent for it. He had invented a machine which held the shoe on the last, gripped and pulled the leather down around the heel, set and drove in the nails, and then discharged the completed shoe.

Garrett A. Morgan
(1875–1963)

Garrett A. Morgan, inventor of the first automatic stop signal, was born in Paris, Tennessee, during the Reconstruction period. In 1895 he moved to Cleveland, Ohio, where he produced his first invention, a belt fastener for sewing machines, in 1901. In 1914, at the Second International Exposition of Sanitation and Safety, he won the First Grand Prize gold medal for his invention of a smoke inhalator.

In 1916, Morgan proved the usefulness of the inhalator by rescuing workmen trapped in a tunnel under Lake Erie; he was awarded a gold medal by the city of Cleveland. He sold the patent rights to his stop signal for $40,000.

John Henry Murphy
(1840–1922)

John Henry Murphy, founder of *The Baltimore Afro-American* newspaper, was born a slave in Baltimore but was emancipated in 1863. He enlisted in the Union Army and served as a noncommissioned officer during the last years of the Civil War.

Murphy learned the printing trade late in life; until he was 50 years old, he worked at many menial trades. The turning point in his life came when he launched his Baltimore Afro-American newspaper, for which he set the type himself and delivered the first issues. At the time of his death, this venture had developed into one of the largest Negro newspapers in America, printed in a plant manned and operated entirely by Negro employees. Murphy exemplified the type of leader who firmly believed in the ability of the Negro people to succeed, as he himself had done, even after many years of disappointment and frustration.

Robert Purvis
(1810–1898)

Robert Purvis, businessman and abolitionist, was born in Charleston, South Carolina. He was educated in Philadelphia and at

Amherst, from which he was graduated. Although he was heir to his wealthy father's fortune and appeared to be white, he worked for, and identified with, the Negroes. He married a daughter of James Forten, with whom he had worked in the antislavery movement.

Two years after William Lloyd Garrison founded *The Liberator,* Purvis helped organize the American Anti-Slavery Society and the Pennsylvania Anti-Slavery Society, but he devoted most of his time and effort to the Underground Railroad. Purvis defied the Federal Fugitive Slave Law by belonging to state vigilance committees which aided escaping slaves; and, as a prominent member of the Negro convention movement, he fought for the amendments to give Negroes suffrage and the right to serve on juries and to join the militia.

Norbert Rilleux
(1806–1894)

Norbert Rilleux, famous engineer and inventor, was born in Louisiana, but he was sent to France to be educated. Upon his return to New Orleans, he became interested in finding a solution to the problem of refining sugar, because the old "Jamaica train" method was slow and costly.

In 1846, Rilleux developed a vacuum pan that revolutionized the method of refining sugar and reduced the production cost of granulated sugar, which still retained its sweetness but now lost its crude, dark color. Although other scientists had developed similar vacuum pans and condensing coils, they had failed to utilize the heat properly during the evaporating process. Rilleux solved this problem by enclosing the condensing coils in a vacuum chamber and by adding a second chamber for evaporating the juice under greater negative pressure.

Rilleux also designed a method for handling sewage which could have removed the menace of yellow fever from New Orleans, but his scheme was not adopted.

Moses Rodgers
(? –1890)

Moses Rodgers, mining engineer and owner of several mines in California, was born a slave in Missouri. He seized every opportunity he could to obtain an education, giving special attention to mathematics and engineering. Arriving in California in 1849 at the peak of the gold rush, he was highly successful in working his claims. With his gold, he was able to purchase mines. To establish his family where the children could be educated, he built an attractive house in Stockton, where, boring for a gas well, he spent thousands of dollars until he finally reached the source.

Moses Rodgers was an expert in his line, and his opinion was always sought by would-be purchasers of mines. He was a man of honor, and his word was as good as his bond.

David Ruggles
(1810–1849)

David Ruggles, one of the first men of African blood to escape slavery, was a daring conductor on the Underground Railroad. He was reported to have helped more than 600 slaves to escape from the southern states to the North and Canada. Along with his work on the Underground Railroad, Ruggles struggled for the moral, social, and political elevation of the free Negroes of the North. He published, in 1838, the quarterly magazine *The Mirror of Liberty,* which advocated the rights of the Negro. This was the first magazine to be edited by a Negro.

Ruggles also owned a bookstore and had a reputation as a hydrotherapist. He had his own establishment for water cures at Northampton, Massachusetts.

Granville T. Woods
(1856–1910)

Granville T. Woods, inventor of electrical appliances, was born in Columbus, Ohio, where he worked in a machine shop while studying privately and attending evening school. In 1872, Woods was employed as a fireman and engineer on a railroad in Missouri, but he continued with his studies in electrical and mechanical engineering.

After settling in Cincinnati, he opened a factory for the manufacture of telephone, telegraph, and electrical equipment. In 1884 he introduced his first invention, a steam-boiler furnace. His next productions were an amusement apparatus, an incubator, and automatic air brakes. He patented more than 15 devices for electrical railways and a telegraphic device for transmitting messages between moving trains. Eventually, Woods moved to New York, where he continued to produce devices for the large electrical manufacturers.

*   *   *

Men like these are giants who paved the way for their race in business and industry. It is not generally known that many blacks have made important contributions to the technological development of our country. For example, Negroes were awarded 347 patents during the years 1871 to 1900. Their inventions range from an electrical railway system to corn-husking machines to refrigerators to rotary machine lubrication. Let's look at what present-day blacks are doing with that heritage.

PART TWO

Recruiting

INTERVIEWS

Durant Brockett

Durant Brockett has formed Achievement Consultants, Inc., Corona, New York, to aid both black and white clients in corporations in personal growth, development, and self-motivation. He has concentrated his efforts in sales organizations.

In this way, Brockett believes, he is doing something direct and positive to help members of his race, which hitherto has only sparsely populated executive and sales jobs in business and industry. Achievement Consultants is a franchised operation which he purchased from the Success Motivation Institute of Waco, Texas.

Brockett says that "intelligence is not measured by the number of degrees an individual has, but by how quickly he can adapt to any situation or problem and bring about an equitable solution." He believes that the basic problem of minority groups is lack of self-image, determination, and self-confidence. "All of us have an abundance of talents and abilities," he says. "The average individual uses only 25 to 35 percent of his total potential. Through positive thinking on a daily basis, our present percentage of usable talents and abilities can be increased. The end result will be to achieve the success we desire—tangible or intangible."

The basic purpose of Achievement Consultants is to motivate people to their full potential through repetitive exposure to positive ideas on a daily basis. His programs also teach how to set long- and short-range goals and how to achieve them. He points out that the three common denominators for success are a positive mental attitude, goal orientation, and self-motivation. "Once an individual attains these success habits," Brockett believes, "his goal achievement is only a matter of time. It is imperative that the black man have confidence in himself. He must believe he is born equal with an equal opportunity to become unequal. There is an abundance of opportunity available to all of us. Unless we are aware of these opportunities, we shall continue to be lost in the shuffle."

Obviously, Brockett is optimistic by nature. And he's more optimistic than some of his race about the future of the Negro in white-collar jobs. He tells his fellow blacks, "Don't fear the white man. Act as if, and believe, he is your equal. The white man always acts superior until he is disarmed by a black man who is affluent and/or highly intelligent." He expresses a similar positive philosophy with this advice to his "brothers" on how to get a managerial or professional job: "Seek and ye shall find."

Brockett does not think that the characteristics essential to the Negro manager or professional differ a jot from those required for the white manager or professional. Nor does he face any special problems in business that do not confront most whites in the white-collar ranks. And, of course, he finds no significant difference between dealing with whites in business and dealing with members of his own race. As could be expected, he strongly believes that present managers should treat Negro white-collar employees the same as any other white-collar employees.

Brockett offers this advice to present white managers and professionals for better relationships with their black colleagues:

1. Stop thinking in terms of superiority to blacks.
2. Attain empathy and communication.
3. Shake off the fear of having to take orders from blacks. ("The day is here!")
4. Award promotions, raises, and pay on the basis of performance only.

As far as promotion is concerned, Brockett wants equal treatment from present management. He asks for advancement criteria "weighted on the basis of a human being only and on honest evaluations."

Before going into business for himself, Brockett worked for

others for a decade in various capacities with firms in the New York area. He has been in engineering, construction, and petrochemicals. But he is now in sales, because "sales is the key to our economy and it is also the most lucrative profession."

Brockett cites hard work, efficiency, and education as musts in preparing for the office environment. His own education includes stints at Howard University and New York University, where he studied mechanical and electrical engineering.

Brockett was born on July 20, 1938, in Jamaica, New York. He has a son, born in 1960, and a daughter, born in 1963. Although he is confident about the future for blacks in white-collar fields, he does not believe it proper for parents to "sway their children to follow in their footsteps." He does say, "Let them see how life is for us."

Brockett's final advice to the "brothers" is: "Never give mental recognition to defeat, and don't look back unless you intend to go there."

Charles H. Butler, Sr.

Can the son of a Pullman porter and a former beauty-shop owner find a spot for himself as a black vice-president of a white-dominated company?

Charles Butler may turn such a Horatio Alger dream into reality. His late father was a Pullman porter, and his mother is a semiretired beautician. Butler began work at the age of 17 with *The New York Times,* where he remained for 14 years (interrupted by two years in the Navy), doing a variety of jobs—messenger, file clerk, credit checker, and advertising-claims adjuster. During that period he went to school nights at New York City Community College, winning an A.A.S. degree in business administration. He went on at Long Island University to acquire his B.S. in business administration in 1962. He is still continuing his education, now aiming to win his master's in public administration at New York University in 1970.

Butler left the *Times* in 1964 for a position as management trainee with the Brooklyn Union Gas Company. He remained there until 1967, when he joined the Endicott Johnson Corporation, having answered an ad in the New York *Amsterdam News* (a black newspaper whose help-wanted advertising has high pulling power among Negroes in the area). He left Endicott Johnson in September 1969 for a better opportunity at the Kennecott Copper Corporation. He frankly aspires to a top management position with Kennecott, where he is now a senior industrial-relations representative.

He sees his major business problem as "trying to convince top management that a black man is capable of holding a nonshowcase top executive job."

Charles Butler believes that present managers can better identify potential managers and professionals among black people through an honest appraisal system and by utilizing sound management-development programs. In other words, white managers can best help blacks in the business world in the same way they help white subordinates—"strictly on ability without regard to race."

Butler does not believe that showcase positions for black people will help them in the long run. He pleads for genuine jobs. He advises, "If a job does not offer a future, obtain all the necessary experience from it and then move on to one that does." He points out that the company that has already demonstrated "a sincere interest in the black community" will have a much easier time recruiting capable Negroes than one whose actions in this area have not shown as much zest as its words. He recommends professional placement firms that specialize in black people to both Negroes and businesses seeking more minority-group members in their white-collar ranks.

To potential black members of the white-collar ranks, Butler suggests that they take quality courses in college, be honest with themselves and their colleagues, and learn the characteristics of a successful executive so that they can develop them in their own personality. He believes honesty is the key attribute.

He points out that a black person may have trouble being realistic in the business world, because his background and experiences may give an emotional bias to his judgment. Although the white-dominated company may have its biases and emotional hang-ups, it can't flourish over the long run without a substantial measure of realism. That is one reason why Charles Butler places such importance on honesty and realism in individuals as well, and it is why he thinks, also, that there should be no double standards in the way present managers treat white-collar employees.

Butler believes in the "living witness" principle—that "those who have made it should come back and tell the brothers and sisters 'like it is.'" Once a black person has won a white-collar job, he can aspire to top positions "by taking advantage of tuition-refund and executive-development programs, participating in community relations activities, and joining professional clubs and societies."

Butler relies on honesty in winning over some of the white associates with whom he deals. "Authentic facts and figures will usually persuade them to my point of view," he says. For example: "Before submitting a report or making a statement to top management, I make sure that I check and double-check my facts and figures, because even the most infinitesimal mistake will tend to leave a credibility gap. I can recall an incident at Endicott Johnson. A top-ranking executive did question some figures which I submitted in a report. My boss confronted me with this, but luckily I had all my source documents to back up my figures (which were correct). I was never questioned again on any of my reports."

Butler was born in 1932 in the Bronx, New York City. He is married and has two sons.

Gerald A. Challenger

"Top management in a company must arrive at a decision before that company will make what is an apparently sincere attempt at achieving racial integration among white-collar employees. But too often that decision doesn't become effectively implemented by the lower-ranking managers who do the hiring," believes Jerry Challenger. He continues: "More accurately, there are probably few companies whose top management is sincere in this regard; compliance with federal standards is usually the purpose, and sincerity is measured in terms of that company's business interests. Implementation at the lower-ranking level is a function of how far behind that company may be in its effort."

Challenger draws such conclusions from experiences in New York and California, where he has worked in electronics, and now group insurance, with multibillion-dollar companies.

His first advice for white managers and professionals "is to get the message on integration all the way up and down the white-collar line—that regardless of the vehicle, black professionals are intent on grasping every opportunity to get ahead in American business." Next, he advises them to "demand the same measure of excellence from us as they do from a white person—and to express the same appreciation for good work—by rewarding effort as well as accomplishment and by paying blacks the same as whites: according to performance."

For young black men and women aiming at white-collar work in business and industry, he suggests they look first at the consumer and finance fields. "Consumer work places blacks in the public eye," Challenger points out. "We need to be seen by people as capable of discharging our responsibilities effectively. In finance, we must win the confidence of the white community that we're accurate, careful, and reliable."

For the same purpose—exposure—Challenger suggests these professions as the most desirable for Negroes because blacks need more inroads in these areas: data processing, banking, consumer and industrial sales, advertising, pharmaceuticals, and cosmetics. He believes that the northeastern and northwestern parts of the nation are "most hospitable for the ambitious black man or woman, but the remaining parts of the country are in desperate need of black professional recognition."

Jerry Challenger reminds blacks who presently hold white-collar jobs that they have responsibilities toward other Negroes who aspire to such work. "Set a good example of professional composure and the ability to lead others," he advises. "Private counseling of fellow blacks concerning employment opportunities, and occasional hints to one's employer that young blacks would be well suited for newly created positions, can frequently open broad lines of communication."

As the father of two young children, a son and a daughter, Challenger will advise them to have business experience when they grow up and finish college. "Business is a team effort," he points out, "and it's valuable for a youngster to learn how teamwork is accomplished, because the lesson will aid him regardless of what he eventually chooses for his life's work."

He goes on to offer this advice to the young aspirant to a white-collar job: "Avoid rigidity, remain flexible, digest fundamentals, broaden interests, keep abreast of current events, make as many friends as possible, and remain poised." Challenger lists such precepts so that the youngster "can meet any career in business on a firm footing, free from insecurity. Knowledge and confidence will permit him to cope with any new environment."

He comments: "In the course of relaxed conversations, I do not find a guarded or hostile atmosphere among my white subordinates or coworkers, either in the choice of topics or in their opinions on urban problems. I am not deluded into thinking that prejudices do not exist, but I do encourage free exchange and inquiry, because understanding can emerge only after intelligent, candid discussion has taken place. It has been my experience that many whites have questions they would like to have firsthand answers to but are hesitant to ask. I feel that giving sound, tempered answers is the responsibility of every black, so that the next black may have a welcome reception in the business environment."

Challenger wishes that the racial question were absent in business, but agrees it is not. "My race has unquestionably hindered my advancement," he says. Although there is no way to be sure, he looks at white men doing work comparable to his and estimates that they make 10 to 20 percent more than he does.

Challenger was born in 1936 in New York City but has lived in California since 1969. His father is a television repairman and his mother a housewife. Challenger has been working toward a degree at City College of New York; at first, he aimed for a B.S. in electrical engineering, but he has since changed his sights and now intends to remain in some phase of insurance work.

Pierre A. Dillard

"There is one problem I face in business that does not confront most whites. That is a conscious or subconscious discounting of my qualifications because of my blackness. This discounting is most damaging during initial contacts and interviews for positions. It has had the effect of forcing me to have more education and experience for a given position in comparison to the average white applicant."

So says Pierre Dillard, who since January 1970 has been with the Stone & Webster Co. in New York as a pipe-stress analyst in its piping-mechanical department. His duties involve the special design of piping and piping-system components for petrochemical process plants, in addition to piping flexibility stress analysis, pipe-support planning, and production.

Dillard has faced this discounting several times in his career. He started as a civil-service employee for the U.S. Department of the Navy. For five years—from July 1957—he worked in the Public Works Department's Design Division as a student-trainee in a cooperative scholarship program under which he went to Pratt Institute in Brooklyn part of the time and worked for the federal government the rest. After receiving his bachelor's degree, he continued in the civil-service job for two and a half years as a mechanical engineer. Next, he moved over to the Treadwell Corporation in New York City to become a mechanical design engineer. For more than a year, he designed fume- and dust-control systems for metallurgical plants. He switched again in January 1966, this time to the Parsons-Jurden Corporation in New York, where he did much the same work as at Treadwell.

To overcome job-interview problems, Pierre Dillard says, "I try to be straightforward in my approach regarding my background and what I feel I am worth, considering the company and current salary trends. I also ask for frankness in replies to my questions about possibilities for advancement in job responsibility."

From his experience with the job interview, Dillard points out that "it can only reveal so much. Invariably, it takes some time on the job to find out what the situation actually is as it relates to you." He believes this takes longer for a black than for a white—"time which can't be recovered and is therefore costly." He adds, "I indirectly offset the discounting by trying to make a good impression so that, hopefully, those blacks following me may be better received."

Pierre Dillard lists these characteristics as most important in his career:

1. Objectivity—"which made it possible for me to decide at an early age what career I wanted."
2. Perseverance—"which enabled me to maintain my stride toward my goals."
3. A sense of humor—"which enables me to remain objective during times of stress and acts as a balancing influence when I begin to take setbacks too seriously."
4. Self-confidence—"which helps me formulate solutions to problems."

He likes the cooperative approach to education for a career which he followed at Pratt and the Public Works Department, and he recommends it for others. He advises the black applicant for a job to follow the conventional avenues for white and black—classified ads, employment agencies, personal contacts, college placement services, letters to potential employers—but he also advocates use of special routes for blacks, notably civic organizations and black employment agencies.

Dillard believes that comparatively numerous minority-group members now qualify for managerial or professional positions but don't hold them. "They have had to settle for something less."

He suggests that business and industry develop more clear-cut criteria for selecting managers and professionals. Obviously, he believes that such criteria should not include racial or ethnic characteristics. He suggests that standards take into account ability, not seniority, and the potential for incentive that promotion to a managerial or professional job holds for the individual. Dillard thinks that many promotions mistake financial need for such incentive. He points out: "Sometimes, the procedure by which managers (and professionals) are selected falls short of logic. This makes discounting more likely.

"But," he adds, "in setting up these clear-cut criteria and procedures for selection, definite steps should be taken to seek and select blacks with potential. This might involve starting and continuing company-sponsored educational programs and assignments geared toward making all criteria relevant to blacks."

Pierre Dillard was born on October 16, 1940, in New York City. His father is a professional musician. His mother, now dead, was a housewife. He is married and has two young sons. He believes in continuing education and will receive his master's degree in mechanical engineering at the Polytechnic Institute of Brooklyn in June 1970. He plans to continue his education by attending lecture series offered by technical societies, and he also plans to take a course from time to time at one of the colleges in New York.

Dillard hopes to go into business for himself someday, possibly in home construction. In preparation for this goal, he intends to work his way into higher levels of engineering management in industry.

Norman M. Johnson

"Black is fashionable and should be capitalized on at this time," says Norm Johnson. The American Airlines personnel representative and assistant chairman for Tulsa's Employers Association for Merit Employment (TEAM) wryly refers, of course, to skin color, not clothing fashions. He believes that Negroes' economic salvation lies in business and industry, not in teaching, government, or the other traditional "black" professions in which most of the more prosperous of his race once made their living. Not that the traditional fields will cease to attract many Negroes; it's just that business and industry are where more good job opportunities lie and "where the money is to be made."

Johnson believes that greater financial prosperity will provide the key by which blacks will unlock many doors often closed to them now —especially in housing and education.

Although he may sound cynical in urging Negroes to capitalize on "fashionable black," Johnson also thinks that "each man should be on his own and not rely on help from others—black or white." He points out that the Negro community must erase some of the anti-business feeling it holds—emotions that stem from years of discrimination against blacks in management and professional jobs by many, though not all, enterprises. The white business establishment can further this cause by showing its sincerity, "being objective, not allowing prejudices to interfere with personnel judgments, and looking at people as individuals with certain skills and experiences to offer, not as specific types." Above all, he says, it must "treat blacks as employees, not as black employees."

To a young Negro considering a business career, Johnson would recommend engineering, computer sciences, or both as a career, provided he has abilities and interests in those areas, because "this is where the most critical need is, especially for blacks." He adds that "many companies need engineers and programmers."

Norm Johnson was born in 1930 in the city of Albia, Iowa, where he attended public school and graduated from high school in 1947. He spent three years in the 82d Airborne Division as a paratrooper and court reporter. After his discharge from the armed forces, he attended Drake University in Des Moines. There he participated in football and track. He received his B.S.E. in January 1955 and has since done graduate work at Drake University, Tulsa University, and Benedictine Heights.

Norm had a brief fling with the Los Angeles Rams before an injury to his leg made it necessary for him to give up football. While with the Rams, he recalls, he had long talks with the late Eugene Liscomb, his roommate. Gene was especially "paternal" on the football field, always seeking to help his little friends, whom he always called "Little Daddy"—thus "Big Daddy" came naturally as his nickname.

Johnson returned to Des Moines in 1955 and taught school for the next two years. He moved to Tulsa, Oklahoma, in September 1957 to accept an assignment as teacher and coach for the Tulsa public schools, where he spent the next six years. In September 1963, he returned to Iowa and worked for Deere & Company until May 1965, when he returned to Oklahoma to accept employment with North American Rockwell. This is where he received his introduction to personnel work. He worked there as a personnel services coordinator until May 1967, when he went to American Airlines.

Norm's present job title is "personnel and employment representative." His work now includes hiring in unskilled, skilled, clerical, and professional areas at American's Maintenance and Engineering Center in Tulsa, and he is a company representative for various agencies and projects. He also coordinates the NAB/JOBS program.

Norm Johnson is the father of five children by previous marriages. He and his present wife, Elena, were recently married.

Philip E. Jones

How can Negroes get white-collar jobs? "By being lucky and using every employment device available to them, including militancy, trickery, and subterfuge."

That's the bitter answer of Phil Jones. Perhaps he is especially "cynical" (as he describes it) because he is in the employment business. Jones is an executive development officer with Marine Midland Grace Trust Company in New York City. He works in recruitment, selection, and training of management associates and development of all officers of the bank.

Phil Jones believes that most blacks in white-collar work have to be more than qualified for the job and "white-minded." By that, he means that a Negro may look black, but he has to act and think like a white man to win advancement with most employers.

In his opinion, a white can get a white-collar job "just by being around." He concedes that there are white people "who are truly qualified," but he charges that they face nothing like the obstacles facing a black. A black, for example, can't afford "to make waves" in

48

his white-collar job, while a white can usually risk at least some gentle rocking of the boat.

Phil Jones argues that some of the problems for the black man in white-collar jobs will fade if, simply, more of them get such positions. And, when more join the ranks, more will be better prepared for the office environment. He draws attention to an often-overlooked fact: There is presently not much tradition among Negroes for white-collar work in business and industry. Consequently, a disproportionately small part of the black population seriously aspires to it. Yet, if the white-collar tradition gets started among black people, more will aim for office work, and a snowball effect will start which can bring a dramatic change.

Phil Jones does not believe that the black man will break down the present barriers to white-collar employment by trying to be white in every way except skin pigmentation. "Be black," he advises. "Add new dimension to white-collar ranks." He thinks business and industry can profit and broaden their perspectives by getting the true black viewpoint.

He acknowledges that in today's social climate some blacks can win good white-collar jobs because of their color. Phil Jones doesn't begrudge them their jobs, but he cautions that, essentially, they owe these jobs to an unnatural situation. He hopes that Negroes who get such work because of the accident of their color will make their greatest contribution by preparing the white-collar ranks for the increasing influx of black people.

Jones offers this advice to white managers who sincerely wish to identify blacks as potential managers or professionals: "Enlist the aid of professional, psychologically oriented specialists to help overcome prejudices. Be fair. Accept leadership ability and skill regardless of color. Learn to motivate employees regardless of color."

Jones was born on June 23, 1936, in New York City. His father is a real estate salesman and his mother a housewife. He holds a B.S. degree from New York University, which he attended nights, majoring in speech. He received that degree in 1966, ten years after getting an A.A.S. degree from New York City Community College.

Most of his professional experience has been in the employment fields—with the YMCA's Sloane House, where he gave information about employment practices and opportunities in the New York area; with New York University's placement service; and with the Metropolitan Life Insurance Company, where, among many duties, he developed college-relations programs for recruiting at traditionally Negro colleges. He has also worked for an employment firm, Stowell, Hauser and Associates.

Jones has put his speech education to good use in countless speaking engagements. He has participated in many campus visits for College Placement Services, Inc., and has also served as metropolitan coordinator for the Vice President's Task Force on Youth Motivation.

Phil Jones belies the "cynicism" of his views on how a Negro can get a white-collar job by also pointing out that the key is "work, work, work like hell."

Jim White

"Learn how to fight in the corporate 'jungles,' " Jim White advises black people who want to progress in managerial or professional jobs in business and industry. White, a manager of educational relations with Honeywell, Inc., in Minneapolis, believes that Negroes who have had to fight for progress most of their lives find themselves ironically handicapped in this different kind of battle. It's a gentlemanly kind of struggle, he thinks, for which most black people find themselves peculiarly ill prepared. He makes these comments:

"Black people must learn how to be aggressive, stoke up their ambition, and develop the techniques of in-fighting—how to come up with new ideas, how to guard their own positions, how to associate with people who can help them. They must know how to walk a fine and sensitive line between aggression and tact, between persuasion and manipulation."

The characteristics essential to the Negro manager or professional, Jim White believes, "are basically the same as for whites, except that the black man must be more aggressive and at the same time more tactful than a white man has to be." He suggests that blacks ambitious for advancement in the white-collar ranks should "take more courses in business administration and psychology in college, participate in in-service management courses, get exposure to as much business experience as possible, and keep everlastingly at the process of education, both on the job and in formal courses in universities."

White suggests to present management that they can hire more black employees by "using more Negro employment agencies and management consultants."

Jim White's experience with Honeywell has not convinced him that there are many minority-group members now qualified for managerial or professional positions who do not hold them. "There are some; however, I doubt that they are numerous." He suggests that industry make "special efforts to find bright, ambitious black men and women and follow up with intensive training programs." In his educational job with Honeywell, he is responsible for such training, among other things. He also administers a program with five public schools which Honeywell has "adopted." White is in charge of helping to determine major contributions to various civic organizations, and he also discharges some Equal Employment Opportunity responsibilities.

Jim White obtained his Honeywell position directly from the president, who hired him. Jim had read a Chamber of Commerce speech by the president on human relations, had been impressed by it, and had written requesting an interview.

He had been in the teaching profession ever since he graduated from Wiley College in Marshall, Texas, and completed graduate work in education at the University of Southern California in Los Angeles. The profession runs in the family, because his father is a retired college professor. Jim White had intended to remain in secondary public schools, having held high school teaching positions in Dallas, Los Angeles, and Winnipeg, Manitoba, and British Columbia, Canada.

Now that he's in industry, he sees the potential for teaching young people in business. He likes the outlook and the attitude there. "Some of the most dramatic experimentation in the field of teaching," he believes, "is going on today among American corporations." He sees himself as continuing in the profession he long ago chose for himself, although he did not at first expect his employer to be a private enterprise. He hopes to continue in industry and wants to pick up some line experience to broaden his background and chances for advancement.

Jim White was born in 1928. Married, he is the father of three young children.

Lowell Thomas

"One way to prepare our black people better for the office environment at clerical and comparable levels is by giving good-quality education, equal to that given whites," says Lowell Thomas. He adds that the office-employment openings have to be provided once the education is acquired.

When Negroes have undertaken white-collar jobs, employers can help them to aspire to top positions by showing that the company has a merit system and by encouraging them when work is well done. He cautions employers, however: Don't promote for mere tokenism; treat your black white-collar employee as an individual, not as a member of a minority group.

To recruit properly, he feels, companies should go into the Negro communities and establish offices for recruitment, working through churches, schools, and social agencies.

Imperative to the black manager or professional, in Thomas's opinion, are the ability to learn rapidly and the ability to handle himself well in conducting business with others. The personal characteristics that he thinks most important to his own career are his skill, experience, and imagination on job assignments. He has been a map and architectural draftsman for the past six and a half years with the Chicago Department of Urban Renewal, and he has been seeking a job in industry which will provide sound wages and benefits and a good training program for future progress.

When asked if he believes there are numerous minority-group members now qualified for managerial or professional positions who do not hold them, he replies, "I would be inclined to say yes. I think they do not necessarily have to have a degree to hold these positions, but they must have a background of some experience in the field—although a degree helps." This feeling led him to go back to night school at the Illinois Institute of Technology, where he has earned two and a half years of college credits in architectural design.

Present managers can better identify potential professionals and managers by looking for experience and quality of work among both college graduates and nongraduates. The latter in particular, Thomas believes, should have shown potential in training programs. He says it is up to the employer to administer equitable hiring and promotional, salary, and benefit practices for black employees. Judging from his experience and observation, he thinks most professional black employees function well with both their white and their black associates.

Lowell was born in 1938 in Chicago and is married. His mother was a clerk and his father an electrician.

John Walker

John Walker is concerned about the problem of "super Negroes." By this term he means the need for the black man or woman to be superqualified and supercapable if he is to be promoted readily.

"We are what we are," says the assistant manager for the Chemical Bank, who specializes in administrative and operational work. "Most whites can attain what they want with a bachelor's degree," he points out. "They are given a chance in some position to see if they like it. They needn't be too aggressive or dynamic, or have the gift of gab."

Walker holds such views because he applied without success for training program after training program before he finally won a position with Chemical Bank in April 1965. He still thinks he's a little out of place in the white business world. "I feel they don't know what to do with me or don't know where I will fit in best," he comments. For the black with conventional qualifications, "fitting in" can be a big problem, he believes—even though he doesn't like the expression. What it really connotes, he says, is a question: "Whose toes will be stepped on if the average Negro is put into the wrong place?"

Walker wants the best candidate to win the job, but he says that present managers often don't even consider black aspirants. "Present managers must remove the blinders and see this and provide the opportunity," he urges. "They must take a chance. They must move more blacks into responsible positions. Then they'll see motivation like they've never seen it before."

The characteristics essential for a Negro who wants to be a successful manager or professional "should be the same as for whites," John Walker believes. "But, realistically, they must be higher for the black man—the highest amount of education possible, at least a master's. He must be more aggressive, have the gift of gab, and know what he's aiming for."

Therefore, Walker continues with his own education. He holds a B.S. in business administration from Wilberforce University and is currently attending Long Island University, where he plans to complete studies for a master's degree in management. In addition, he has taken advantage of every educational opportunity that presented itself to him—training programs, free tuition for school, and further study as an assistant manager.

Walker hopes to continue with the bank in administrative or personnel work, perhaps becoming a vice-president someday. Before joining Chemical Bank, he spent more than five years with Wm. M. Tynan & Company, Inc., a meat-brokerage firm in New York, where he was head bookkeeper.

Perseverance and optimism are the characteristics Walker feels have been most important in his career. That optimism leads him to this realistic hope: "I feel that changes are happening so fast that white Americans will eventually feel that no more is required of blacks than whites."

Walker points out a related anomaly which he hopes will soon disappear: He finds it easier to manage or deal with white associates in business than with members of his own race. "Until we can say we've all got it made," he says, "blacks will be jealous of blacks and will therefore give each other a harder time."

John Walker was born in York, South Carolina, in 1933. His father is a fireman and his mother a retired schoolteacher. He moved to New York in 1955 from New Jersey because of the occupational opportunities the big city offers. He's married and is the father of a son, born in 1959, and a daughter, born in 1962.

DISCUSSION

The key to recruiting Negroes for managerial and professional jobs is this: Avoid practices that screen people out; develop practices that screen them in.

Ulric Haynes, Jr., a business-oriented Negro who heads Management Formation, Inc., a firm that specializes in recruiting black people for industry, says: "What the concept of aptitude testing ignores is that the prevailing patterns of discrimination exclude minority-group members from the very experiences on which aptitude tests are based." And the screening out goes beyond aptitude testing.

Many an employer hiring a potential manager or professional wants the applicant to have a college degree in or near the specialty for which he is hiring—business administration, for example, or the appropriate engineering area. Yet most college-educated blacks today come from Negro institutions, and few of these offer degrees in business administration, and few offer even engineering courses. This is changing—both because the black schools are broadening their curricula and because more Negroes are entering white institutions—but the situation inhibits the recruiting now. That's why Ted Nims urges more business courses in Negro colleges.

Nims also puts his finger on another, more subtle cause of "screening out." He says, "The average Negro college student still doesn't picture blacks in such fields as marketing." Negroes may screen themselves out here, but businessmen often contribute to the problem by not trying very hard to recruit blacks for marketing, administrative, and related positions. The National Association of

Market Developers, an association of Negroes in marketing, has long complained about this situation. It goes so far as to charge major American concerns with "systematically ignoring" Negroes when they recruit for such positions. Jonathan Nelson describes the results of such practices: "An alarmingly large number of black people," he says, "still do not believe that industry is truly sincere when it claims not to discriminate with respect to hiring and advancement."

Catch-as-catch-can recruiting results in screening out many blacks. For example, the company that confines its recruiting to occasional help-wanted ads in metropolitan dailies or white-oriented national magazines won't draw many responses from Negroes. As Durant Brockett and many others point out, blacks don't put much faith in ads in white papers. In short, the business recruiter has to plan his approach to be sure he will find qualified Negroes. The experienced recruiter, of course, knows that planned techniques are the only sure-fire methods for getting good results—with whites or blacks.

Some of those interviewed acknowledge that the "checkered careers" of a number of blacks may screen them out of consideration for a professional or managerial job with a new employer. However, as Bill Outlaw explains, the explanation for some Negroes' checkered backgrounds is that they couldn't win promotions with previous employers. He and others advise white recruiters to discount job hopping as a sign of instability in a black candidate. It's more likely to be a sign of racial discrimination, they claim.

Gerald Challenger draws attention to still another facet of the "screening out" process—top management directives to hire blacks often are not implemented by middle managers after they have been filtered through several levels. "Get the message all the way up and down the white-collar line," he urges.

The screening-out process continues when management hires blacks only for special kinds of jobs or hires only blacks with exceptional skills. Bernard Walker advises: "Take blacks out of the 'special' category." They are people just like whites, he emphasizes. He and others interviewed express doubts about the public-relations and urban-affairs jobs now held by so many Negroes; these jobs may be self-defeating for their race. John Walker lodges a related complaint: The hunt for "super" Negroes, the kind so often portrayed by Sidney Poitier. Roscoe Robinson, an electronics technician, describes the problem: "When people find that I don't meet their stereotype for *the*

Negro who has made it into an exclusive field, they figure I have just faked my way in and have made it on luck. They try to treat me accordingly." Such condescension screens some blacks out.

How, then, can businessmen minimize this screening out? We suggest the following techniques:

1. Plan your recruiting.
2. Know what jobs you're recruiting for.
3. Know the kind of people you want.
4. Know where and how to find the people you want.
5. Advertise your interest in black candidates.
6. Know what blacks want from industry.
7. Know what blacks want from recruiters.
8. Know how to interview blacks.
9. Sell blacks on business.
10. Know the techniques of selection.

Of course, many of the recruiting approaches we shall describe are desirable regardless of race, but differences do exist for Negroes, particularly in emphasis and focus. For example, a company with few blacks in white-collar positions will find it difficult, although not impossible, to make a breakthrough. Therefore, it must make special efforts to prove to Negro candidates that it is changing its ways.

Another instance of the differences needed in recruiting blacks: You will probably make more points with Negroes than with whites if you can offer a well-proved training program for managers or professionals. This situation comes about because blacks recognize their greater need for training. Furthermore, many young black adults today have an almost unquenchable thirst for education. If you can offer it, you have a powerful selling point.

With such differences in mind, let's examine the ten techniques.

1. *Plan your recruiting.* You can plan your recruiting only if you know the characteristics of the black people who will seek your white-collar jobs. First, they will likely be young. Older blacks with the education needed for such positions are probably already established, usually in fields outside of business—in education, government, or the professions of law, medicine, and the ministry.

You should aim at Negro youngsters for another reason, too—relatively, there are more of them. The number of young nonwhite adults under 25 years of age in the nation's labor force will increase by 70.9 percent—from approximately 2 million to 3.4 million—between 1965 and 1980, according to predictions of the U.S. Bureau of Labor Statistics. By contrast, the number of young white adults in the same category will increase by only 38.9 percent—from about 14.9 million to 20.7 million—over the same 15-year period.

Superficiality is the particular curse of recruitment practices for blacks seeking white-collar jobs. The complacent assumption that most blacks qualified for such work will leap at your offer is totally false.

Industry does not recruit for black white-collar people in the way that it recruits for whites. Not many recruiters make regular tours of black college campuses, and not many consciously look for blacks in the other schools. All too often, employers recruit young blacks almost by accident. The Negroes happen to be in the recruiting net at some college interviewing session, look promising, and are hired. Only when the employment situation becomes critical do many employers even seriously consider a black youngster. And some of this doesn't stem from racial discrimination. Most companies are unusually selective in hiring *anybody* under 25 years of age. In fact, some employers take young adults only as a last recourse. The reasons for this include the greater cost of training neophytes, the greater chance of mistakes in selecting a relatively unknown and untrained person, the greater possibility that the young person will err in his own selection of a job than if he were older and more experienced, the greater likelihood of job hopping with a young adult than with someone older, and the greater expectations—often unrealistically high—among young adults themselves concerning promotion, pay, supervision, and working conditions.

Some employers recognize their own limitations and avoid young adults—black and white—for reasons such as these: They do not have the necessary training facilities; they do not have supervision qualified to teach; they need, and can somehow attract, older experienced people; the age makeup of the workforce needs seasoning with older people; or they can't, in honesty, offer a young adult a lifetime career.

If any, or several, of these factors exist, the employer probably does young people—white and black—a favor by leaving them to an organization that can handle them. Fortunately, many can. Almost all large companies—and most medium-size ones—are spending increasing time, money, and effort trying to persuade youngsters to join them. Their efforts, however, have not proved spectacularly successful.

In planning your recruiting program, follow the precepts of Jim White, who sums up as follows: Make "special efforts" to recruit blacks—get advice from other companies or consultants with experience in the field, stay flexible so that you can adjust your plan to correct errors, and keep everlastingly at it.

2. *Know what jobs you're recruiting for.* This would appear obvious, but job specifications often prove ambiguous. The simple job designation "foreman" may cover a position requiring the supervision of half a dozen people or a hundred people. And the foreman may supervise unskilled laborers or highly trained technicians. So make your job specifications clear. How many and what kinds of people will the supervisor oversee? Will the professional also be responsible for some managerial work? For example, will the engineer need some administrative experience or training?

Besides making your job specs unambiguous, make them relevant. At least one major company formerly required all supervisors to be 30 or older—a rule whose absurdity becomes clear when you consider that a member of the U.S. House of Representatives need only be 25. Because most of the blacks you recruit for managerial or professional positions will be young, you would screen out the majority of them with such an age specification.

Relevance also has to do with the specifications you make for education and background. Does an office manager have to possess a college degree? Does it matter that a candidate for an engineering drafting job has spent most of his adult life as a common laborer, provided he has somehow acquired the technical expertise to handle the new job?

In professional and semiprofessional job areas, many companies have found excellent candidates even among unlikely members of minority groups. For example, the Federal Systems Division of the International Business Machines Corporation recorded interesting results in a general-skills training program at Huntsville, Alabama. Fourteen students were selected who had the ability but not the educational background to establish careers with IBM. They had worked at such jobs as dishwasher, waiter, delivery boy, and laborer. These students were given a remedial high school course and then began a seven-month work-and-study program that trained them as engineering draftsmen or electronic technicians.

The words "maturity" and "competence" appear frequently in job specifications. Unfortunately, people responsible for picking candidates are prone to give chronological age and educational diplomas undue weight. This is understandable. Such tangible measures are easy to apply against such intangibles as "maturity" and "competence."

In developing specifications for supervisory and professional jobs, then, avoid such vague criteria. More meaningful guides are, for example, "experience" instead of "competence" and "evidence of supervisory ability" instead of "maturity." You will aid black people immeasurably by making such adjustments.

You will also improve your recruiting score if you can offer careers in industries that have most appeal to youngsters. Consumer Research Center, Philadelphia, has surveyed more than 2,700 male juniors, seniors, and graduate students—white and black—to discover their preferences. This and other studies have shown that career objectives today hinge more on age than race: whites and blacks of the same age have similar job aims. And the overwhelming majority of the Negroes you will hire now and for some time in the future will be in the under-25 age group.

This is how the students queried ranked industries as potential employers (the most popular career choice is rated 100, with other ratings indicating relative popularity):

	Rating
Data processing and computers	100
Missiles, space, aeronautics	99
Petroleum	86
Steel and basic metals	84
Banking	78
Drugs and pharmaceuticals	78
Chemicals	77
Automotive industries	74
Rubber and rubber products	66
Textiles, fibers, and garments	58
Insurance	55
Appliances, consumer electronics	49

If you can offer jobs in such fields, you have a leg up. Negroes prefer large and medium-size firms, generally, over smaller companies— apparently because of the superior training opportunities available. However, this preference no longer remains as clear-cut as it once was.

But as Phil Jones puts it: Negroes will try to find white-collar jobs anywhere, "by being lucky and using every employment device available to them." In other words, while they do have preferences, many blacks believe that they still cannot afford to be choosy in the white-collar area.

3. *Know the kind of people you want.* What are the personal characteristics needed for managerial or professional positions? Behavioral research studies have shown that most bright young executives and professionals are serious, aggressive, confident, independent, decisive, inquiring, hard-working, pragmatic, well educated, ambitious, and self-reliant. If these qualities sound too much like those of the ideal Boy Scout, let us point out that the same studies also turn up some disagreeable traits. The young person moving ahead in the managerial or professional ranks often tends to be culturally narrow, rather ruthless toward those he considers his rivals, and overly self-confident—in short, brash.

An awareness of both sides of the personality that you will be attracting will help you plan your approaches to recruiting. However, the good recruiter should remain alert for the occasional nonconformist who may turn out to be an outstanding manager or professional, and the noncomformist will be much more common among black candidates than among white candidates—in fact, being black is itself atypical. Industry must improve its techniques for identifying atypical but promising candidates, if only because there aren't enough typical people coming into business. Even without the pressure of manpower needs, employers would be wise to seek more promising young adults with atypical backgrounds. This would help any company to avoid the dangers of conformity, especially in managerial jobs.

4. *Know where and how to find the people you want.* Jim Walton offers three suggestions on how to recruit more Negroes:

- Recruit more at black schools or at colleges, such as community institutions, with a high proportion of Negroes.
- Use employment agencies specializing in blacks.
- Provide summer jobs for Negroes.

In addition, John Chadwell urges Negroes already holding white-collar jobs to help with recruiting by persuading their qualified friends to apply. Nate King says that whites need "closer personal contacts" with blacks to improve recruiting.

Colleges are the prime source of potential black managers and professionals. Get acquainted with the placement people at Negro institutions, and put at least one such school on your regular recruiting tour. It is not always necessary, though, to visit colleges to recruit graduating students. Recruiting "fairs" during Christmas vacations are becoming increasingly common. Companies pay for booths at such a fair, and interested students may visit them.

5. *Advertise your interest in black candidates.* General Electric did this recently with an ad that began: "There are no whites working at GE. No blacks, either. Just people. And we need more."

Employers can often find young blacks by advertising, particularly in black-oriented media. Many also run help-wanted ads in military publications and in military editions of general magazines in an attempt to attract returning servicemen and women. Often these people do not have college degrees, but they may have the equivalent, or more, from their experiences in managing people and in dealing with technical problems. Furthermore, they may intend to work toward a degree by attending a local institution at night. Peace Corps "graduates" likewise have high potential as managers or professionals, companies have found.

Many companies have extensive summer job programs for college students. These programs are intended to serve a threefold purpose: (1) The student gets to learn something about business in general and the company in particular. (2) The company gets to learn more about the student's potential. (3) The student, in theory, builds up a loyalty toward the summer employer. Summer job programs can prove to be a boon. In Pittsfield, Massachusetts, for example, General Electric administers a summer program for junior and senior students of small, predominantly Negro colleges. Students are selected on the basis of their academic and extracurricular achievement and the compatibility of their field of study with specific, full-time summer positions. Plant tours and various types of meetings, with and without management, provide the students with a broad orientation to the business environment.

On a less ambitious scale, plant tours and open houses may give some blacks a better idea of the office environment. However, these are best relied on only to supplement your other efforts. They will never carry the load alone.

Art White and others interviewed caution against the "sponsorship" route to white-collar jobs. This smacks of paternalism and the "super Negro" problem. Sponsorship is often demeaning for the person sponsored, and from the standpoint of the employer it's an inefficient and slow method of recruiting.

Negroes already in your managerial and professional positions can help by referring their qualified friends. Some companies pay awards for employees brought in—sometimes as high as $500, as for critically needed skills in engineering. Howard Corey believes this route holds special importance for the black people themselves. "Black people must continue to get into influential positions if we are to make it," he points out, arguing that Negroes' self-interest demands that they do more recruiting themselves.

Another solution may be to turn to Negro recruiting organizations. One example is a computerized service offered by two young business school graduates, who match up graduates of Negro colleges with jobs at companies that can't afford to recruit on Negro campuses. Thomas H. Main and his black roommate, Aaron L. Spaulding, graduates of the Wharton School of Finance and Commerce, have founded Re-Con Services, Inc. They screen Negro graduates from 80 black campuses—mostly in the Southeast—to fill job openings. Re-Con got started with several foundation grants. Although most governmental and other institutionalized job-searching organizations concentrate on blue-collar or secretarial positions, some can also provide help in the lower managerial and professional levels—for example, the Urban League's Skills Bank in many localities may offer assistance.

An often-overlooked source of white-collar people is present blue-collar employees. David B. Johnson and James L. Stern, professors of economics at the University of Wisconsin, studied 452 people who had made the switch in Milwaukee County during a two-year period in the early 1960s. The largest number had moved into managerial jobs (39 percent), followed by professional and technical jobs (24 percent), clerical jobs (21 percent), and sales jobs (17 percent).

Although this study was not made on the basis of race, many in the sample were black. Certain characteristics emerged for whites and blacks who made the switch to white-collar positions: Most came from families in which the father had been a blue-collar worker. Shifts came at a fairly early age (31 on the average), and most men making the transfer had a high school education and were married. About 30 percent of them had some full-time higher education but had dropped out of school, usually for financial reasons. A majority had taken part-time schooling after they began work.

The professors make three recommendations to spur shifts from blue-collar to white-collar positions:

- "Employers should give consideration to adoption of formal programs for upgrading blue-collar workers into professional-technical and clerical-sales classifications."
- "Public agencies and employers would do well to perfect their techniques for communicating job openings to job seekers."
- "Better educational and career guidance is needed."

6. *Know what blacks want from industry in management and the professions.* A key to your continued success in attracting well-qualified Negroes lies in offering meaningful jobs with fair pay.

The people interviewed differ somewhat on the so-called showcase jobs. Interviewee Norm Johnson says frankly, "Black is fashionable and should be capitalized on at this time." But he doesn't advise blacks to accept meaningless positions. Those few who do so advise the move as a stepping-stone to something more worthwhile.

Practically everyone interviewed, however, agrees with Charlie Butler that selection, pay, and promotion should be based "strictly on ability without regard to race." Pierre Dillard goes even further in urging business to develop more clear-cut criteria for selection.

In essence, blacks want equity from industry, but their expectations about what constitutes "equity" need study in depth. The most important source of most black candidates for managerial and professional positions remains the college, and the CRC survey of 2,700 students presents revealing facts regarding expectations about a business career. (The study is valid for Negroes even though it includes both white and black respondents.) The students were asked to state what they wanted from a job. Their general areas of response follow (because they were urged to answer as fully as possible, the percentages exceed 100):

64

	Percent
Responses related to work atmosphere, conditions, environment	74
Responses related to work itself, substance of the job	72
Responses related to financial reward, salary	66
Responses related to type of company	8

Under work atmosphere, "chance for advancement" was most often mentioned by the business majors (49 percent). "Job security" was first for liberal arts majors (17 percent), whereas "opportunity to solve problems" was first for science and engineering majors (25 percent). Responses from all the students ranked in this order: job security (19 percent), position of responsibility (13 percent), opportunity to solve problems (11 percent), suitable location (11 percent), position with prestige and status (11 percent), fringe benefits (11 percent), and opportunity to travel (10 percent). Somewhat surprisingly, less than 10 percent of the students considered as important a comfortable environment, opportunity to gain experience, regular working hours, personal work atmosphere, informal (nonbureaucratic) atmosphere, and competent colleagues.

In responses related to the work itself, "interesting, enjoyable, satisfying work" was most often mentioned (by 35 percent of all the students). This was followed by "demanding, challenging work" (19 percent), "work focused on people" (16 percent), and "work involving teaching" (11 percent). Engineering majors, however, failed even to mention this last factor. Less than 10 percent of the total group expressed interest in variety of work, creative work, or intellectual work.

In the area of financial reward, about one-third of the replies had to do with "good salary, money, pay in general." About 20 percent of the group stressed financial stability and security. "A good starting salary" and "a good chance to advance quickly" were mentioned by less than one-tenth of the total group. However, this factor ranked higher with business, science, math, and engineering majors.

As was stated earlier, the students showed a marked preference for the "glamour" businesses, such as data processing and space technology.

The CRC survey also asked the students to rank what they wanted in a job and/or an employer. The results were as follows:

	Percent
Financial reward	100
Work itself	97
Challenge	97
Personal satisfaction	95
Responsibility	93
Advancement	92
Security	85
Variety in work	83
Prestige and status	82
Progressive climate and management	76
Location	76
Fringe benefits	74
Quality of company's product or service	73
Opportunity to travel	71
Well-organized company	68
Informal work atmosphere	65
Conservative management	40

It is clear, then, that students, including Negroes, primarily want financial reward, rewarding and challenging work, personal satisfaction, responsibility, and advancement. In addition, blacks particularly want a larger firm that has status and prestige. If your firm can provide all this, you are a step ahead of the crowd.

7. *Know what blacks want from recruiters.* Black candidates probably prefer black recruiters, but skin color doesn't hold prime importance for most of them. The CRC survey indicates that both white and black students are principally concerned about improvement in recruitment procedures, communication with students, and involvement in students' lives aside from the actual recruitment procedure.

Concerning improvement in procedures, 15 percent of the engineering majors said, "Stop making the student feel you're doing him a favor by talking to him"—the biggest complaint they made. Yet the suggestion most often made by business majors was, "Expand the interview period" (18 percent). Liberal arts majors considered utilizing the interview period for the exchange of more and better information most important (14 percent). Science and math majors said that sending "more and better professionals" to recruit was most important (11 percent).

Concerning improvement in communication, a desire for "more detailed, honest, complete information about jobs and companies" was first among specific responses (23 percent). Students also mentioned these other desires having to do with communication: more "accurate information on jobs" (8 percent); more detailed information about salaries (7 percent), and more information about the company (6 percent), about advancement (5 percent), and about training (3 percent).

Concerning the matter of company involvement in students' lives (aside from actual recruiting), engineering, science, and math majors ranked the offer of summer jobs as of first importance, but business and liberal arts students ranked that a bit lower. Here is how the total group saw the factors (in descending order of importance): Use a more personal touch in dealing with students (letters and so on); offer summer jobs; arrange trips to company headquarters; offer scholarships; deal with students through campus clubs and so on; and show more interest in campus affairs.

8. *Know how to interview blacks.* Your recruiter need not be black, but he should certainly not be prejudiced against blacks. He should know their "language" and remain courteous, respectful, and friendly—not aloof. Above all, he should be neither patronizing nor condescending. Blacks are experts in spotting those two characteristics, and nothing turns them off more quickly.

9. *Sell Negroes on business.* By and large, blacks are not sold on business, as many of the people interviewed indicate. Appeal to what the young people—your prime "market"—want. Despite pious claims to the contrary, all want money. Most potential employees are also concerned about the work itself, the challenge, the responsibility, and the opportunity for advancement: Sell all these if you can. And remember, security is a particularly strong selling point for blacks, because most of them have had so little of it in their lives.

Bill Porter emphasizes that there is now a special opportunity for young blacks to get into management and the professions, because the current disenchantment of some young whites with business provides a partial vacuum which young blacks would be wise to fill.

Katheryn Lawson draws attention to another aspect of this problem. Many blacks may see themselves in industry—but in blue-collar, not white-collar, jobs. They may possess potential for white-collar work, but they never even try for it because it has been off limits to them for decades. Now is the time, she and others advise, to search in the blue-collar ranks for people with white-collar potential. On the other hand, not all people—white or black—want white-collar jobs, she reminds us.

10. *Know the techniques of selection.* Obviously, good recruiting includes good selection. Yet the implications of this are not always followed up, charges Frederic Way, assistant dean in charge of placement at the Columbia University Graduate School of Business. Only since about 1960, he says, have many companies begun to make serious efforts to match men with jobs, "and there are still a lot of firms that don't know what they're doing."

Here are a few basic indicators that shed a revealing light on a candidate's fundamental character.

- *Use of time.* What has he done to broaden himself—what are his hobbies and interests? What has he done with his summers or other vacations? Do his summer or part-time jobs show variety and imagination? For instance, has he had the same stockroom job every summer, or has he tried various things? What books has he read for recreation? Note particularly the range of interests, rather than the quality of the books. Look especially for blanks in the candidate's use of time—times when he just did nothing.
- *Mental competence.* When a man has proved himself on the job, you won't care—or, probably, remember—what grades he got in college. Yet the new man is an unknown quantity. You have to rely on something tangible, and grades are often the only record available. But use them with discretion. Successful businessmen who didn't perform well in school are legion. And blacks, with their different cultural background, may have misleading scholastic records.
- *Ability to communicate.* Here's a way to supplement your impression of mental competence. The better a person can communicate, the better his chances in business and industry. What we mean is not glibness but the ability to articulate an idea or a desire. A black with potential for either a managerial or a professional job should be able to talk and write well. Almost 90 percent of a good manager's job is communicating.

And, while this figure is somewhat lower for the professional, communicating is still usually more than half his job.

Then there is *leadership*. How do you spot this in a brief interview? Many personnel people say you cannot; however, clues usually emerge. For example, what leadership posts did the candidate hold in school? Monte Jacoby, of the Olin Corporation, says, "The important thing is not how many groups he has joined, but what he has done in them—president or chairman of a fraternity or scientific society, captain or manager of a team, editor of the paper, and so on. We want people who've gravitated to the top in whatever they've done."

Once you have established leadership criteria, stick to them. One critic of American management (himself a manager) says, "I think industry really has two sets of criteria—one for what they say they want in young people and the other for what they really want. What they say they want is bright innovators; creative and aggressive, morally and ethically sound people. From what I see, though, I think what they really want is people who can conform, who don't rock the boat."

If you want conformists, you should have no trouble finding them, because there are a lot of them around, white and black. However, even if you want nonconformists, you do not necessarily want the wild revolutionary. The problem of conformity presents great subtleties. Continental Can Company's E. L. Hazard says, "Our society is not threatened by the man in the gray flannel suit. It is threatened by the man with the gray flannel mind, the man who knows method but not meaning, technique but not principle, pragmatic practice but not sound theory—the man of experience who tries to operate in a professional field in which he is unqualified."

Your greatest challenge in selecting good prospects for managerial and professional positions, then, lies in finding people without gray flannel minds—and in having the courage to hire and support them.

PART THREE

Training

INTERVIEWS

Harvey J. Brewster

"Black people in the United States spend approximately $32 billion on consumer goods each year. There isn't any valid reason why black people shouldn't assist in the operation and management of an economy which makes such spending possible," so says Harvey J. Brewster, who is a staff member in the personnel department at Sandia Laboratories in Albuquerque, New Mexico.

Brewster adds that many opportunities are available for Negroes as white-collar workers, and recommends private industry over civil service and the traditional "black jobs"—teaching, preaching, and so forth—because "for black people to broaden their scope of economic success, performance is demanded in all areas of our society." As to professions, he suggests accounting, business administration, personnel administration, computer programming, oceanography, transportation research, marketing, and engineering of all types. "These professions," he points out, "represent just a few of those which black people haven't traditionally cared to pursue or for which they were denied the opportunity to qualify."

Harvey Brewster continues, "Black people can help bring more Negroes into white-collar jobs by explaining to youngsters of high school age the benefits of pursuing a career as a white-collar worker and how to go about preparing for such jobs in college. Black people can also help by encouraging white management to recruit blacks actively for anticipated vacancies. On the job, black people can help Negroes win promotions by explaining how to avoid various job-related obstacles that will face them as white-collar workers. (Listen before you speak!)"

To white managers Brewster gives this advice: "They can help by first reviewing the records of their present black employees to seek out those who are qualifiable for supervisory and professional work and then training these blacks to fill such positions. Secondly, the white managers should actively recruit Negroes for anticipated job openings. Positive action is the most convincing bridge builder toward mutual understanding. After a black man or woman is on the job, white managers can assist in winning promotions by proper guidance and delegation of responsibilities that will test his (or her) willingness to perform a difficult assignment."

Like so many other Negroes, Brewster deplores the window-dressing positions, and he urges blacks to avoid the "traditional bag of 'colored folk' jobs." He points out that there are "hundreds of occupations which make up the economic strength of our society."

Brewster would advise a youngster to start early to pursue a professional or managerial career in business or industry if he has any inclination toward such work. "If the youngster was in his early teens, I would advise exploring the various jobs in a particular field of interest before the junior year in high school, if possible. Finally, I would encourage applying for summer jobs in chosen areas to provide some practical experience before making a final decision."

Harvey Brewster was born in 1935 in Mount Holly, Arkansas, but he considers Muskegon Heights, Michigan, his home town because his parents moved there when he was very young. His father is a semiskilled foundry worker and his mother is a housewife, part-time domestic worker, and student. Brewster himself holds a master's degree from Michigan State University.

After high school, Brewster joined the Air Force and was trained as an X-ray technician. Upon leaving the service in 1958, he entered Michigan State, graduating in 1962. He helped finance his education with an assortment of student jobs—bus boy, library assistant, and so on. After graduation, he worked briefly as a counselor in a detention home for wayward youth. In 1963, he returned to the Air Force, this time as an officer. He stayed in until 1967, emerging as a captain. He is married.

Brewster got his job with Sandia Laboratories by walking into the employment office and applying for it. His duties include personnel counseling and developing, coordinating, and evaluating company policies and programs relating to equal employment opportunities and activities of the National Alliance of Businessmen. He helps coordinate Sandia's various programs with those of other participating firms, educational institutions, and government agencies at all levels. In addition, he spends about 20 percent of his time as a college recruiter for the Bell System, of which Sandia Laboratories is a part. He likes the personnel administration area and hopes to achieve managerial status in it.

His central problem as a black man revolves around the necessity to be a "super black." Allied with this comes a feeling that he must never forget that he is "stage front center" when on the job or in public. "I have learned to live with this," he says, "but the problem is being slowly resolved as other blacks join the white-collar ranks." He says this is also true with respect to housing as more and more Negroes seek and find adequate living quarters.

Brewster believes that his white colleagues' attitudes vary from condescending to friendly. He suggests that "white managers and professionals can promote better relationships with black colleagues by remembering that each of us is an individual." By this he means that whites should avoid the tendency of trying to develop an approach to handle Negroes. "This is a real drag at times," he says. "Whites must come to understand that we blacks have as many ups and downs as the next person."

Alexander Flamer, Jr.

"I think that it is essential for a black man contemplating business as a career to realize that it is definitely an uphill struggle and that he must have the strength to strive continuously for promotion. He must be able to channel hurt into productivity and aggressiveness.

When the door to opportunity opens, he must be standing right next to that door and be ready to step in."

So says Alexander Flamer, Jr., who stood ready to go through the door when it opened for him in 1964 at the Southern New England Telephone Company. With the aid of a scholarship and government loans, he had recently been graduated from Washington and Jefferson College in Washington, Pennsylvania, with a B.A. in languages. Then he had spent a summer in France with the "Experiment in International Living," an experience which convinced him that he wished to continue to live in the United States despite the problems facing the black man in this country.

His mother also works at Southern New England Telephone, as a directory saleswoman. (His father is self-employed in factory maintenance.) Al Flamer started as a coin-telephone consultant, was promoted through several stages of communications positions, and is currently a communications manager. Nine men and three women report to him. His job is a combination of sales training and development, as well as direction of sales operations for profitable coin-telephone locations throughout the state of Connecticut.

"You've got to be a Sidney Poitier (that is, superhuman) at times, to be a Negro manager with some whites reporting to you," he says. By this he means that the black supervisor has to show special skill in handling associates, white and black. "Treat black people like white people. Just be fair," he cautions. "Women, especially white women, are still off limits. It is necessary to be very aware of what happens around you."

Al Flamer gives seven prescriptions for success as a Negro manager or professional:

1. Be a man, but don't be belligerent.
2. Talk like a Philadelphia lawyer.
3. Feel at ease in a white man's world.
4. Know yourself.
5. Develop the patience of Job.
6. Practice flexibility.
7. Don't show bitterness. If possible, channel any hidden bitterness into productivity.

Flamer acknowledges that these seven prescriptions would lead to better managerial health for anyone—white or black—but points

76

out that, while the white manager has some freedom to fail, the Negro usually has less. "The white man can make a mistake and still survive," he believes. He is not certain that he or many black managers can.

Yet he believes that the black man has to earn full equality; it won't come automatically. "A manager must earn the respect of his employees. If he is good, he will have cooperation from blacks and whites."

White managers can help ("I have had some exceptional supervisors") by giving "recognition and constructive criticism, by explaining what is needed to get ahead, by being honest, and by demonstrating a positive attitude in showing that they really want to see Negro advancement."

Al Flamer has some suggestions for Negroes who aspire to white-collar jobs: "Know what's out here—know the realities. Don't dwell on inconsistencies." He elaborates by pointing out that some blacks get overly upset by undeserved promotions or business inefficiencies and practices that seem incomprehensible. The young black novice in the business world tends to expect perfection, perhaps because he has seen so little of it elsewhere. When he doesn't find it in business either, he may overreact and grow bitter and disillusioned.

White managers can forestall such a development if they "tell blacks like it is . . . no b.s. Make them feel like a part of the team."

The Negro, for his part, must "become acquainted with the written and unwritten laws in business, know how to dress, be sociable, and speak well." While Al Flamer admits that these are superficial matters, he advises young blacks not to fight the establishment in this area but to concentrate on more fundamental matters—for example, by persuading " 'Mr. Charlie' that he is going to exercise equal opportunity in the true sense of the word."

Al Flamer was born in 1942 in New Haven, Connecticut. He's married, but he and his wife have no children yet.

Mark Grant

"The first and, so far, the only problem I've encountered," comments Mark Grant, concerning problems he faces in business that don't confront his white colleagues, "was right after I began working. There was only one other Negro programmer on the floor. He was assigned as my mentor, presumably because it was thought that I would feel more comfortable with someone of the same skin pigmentation. The results were disastrous, as we were poles apart in personality, temperament, and work habits."

From 1964 until 1969, Grant was with the Service Bureau Corporation, a wholly owned subsidiary of the International Business Machines Corporation. For the year 1964–65 he was also an evening-session instructor at City College of New York, where he had majored in economics, receiving a bachelor's degree in economics from the Baruch School. He has applied his interest in teaching to his business career; he was responsible for the professional development of programmers and program analysts at the Service Bureau. He is now in Rio de Janeiro as a data processing consultant for International Telephone and Telegraph's South America Computer Division.

Grant was born in 1942 in Jamaica, West Indies, where his father was a machinist and his mother a teacher. All three emigrated to the U.S. in 1952. Now Mark is married and the father of two children.

He believes that "preparation per se is not the problem" as far as advancement in the white-collar ranks is concerned. "The one decisive characteristic that seems essential to the Negro manager or professional is that he must demonstrate superior ability. All evidence indicates that just plain adequacy will not be tolerated from the Negro."

Grant thinks mediocrity is tolerated among whites to a much greater degree than among blacks. The sports world gives a good example of this phenomenon: "Managers, until lately, were quite satisfied with and preferred an inferior white to a superior black. The black athlete who achieved recognition was usually outstanding and dominated his sport." Grant recognizes that business has to tolerate some mediocrity; he merely asks that such toleration be indiscriminate.

"The diseconomies of discrimination," Grant says, "are now reverberating across the United States in rising welfare costs and civil disorder. The solution is equal opportunity. The country would have little trouble reversing some of these disturbing trends if it would recognize the downward-spiraling effect of discrimination: that Negro menials could release thousands of jobs for the hard-core unemployed if they were given an opportunity to enter the various crafts and trades now protected by white unionism. . . . For the most part, the Negro in America is forced to perform at a skill level substantially below his actual potential. All we need is the opportunity."

Grant suggests that white managers can best help Negroes achieve promotions "by just being fair." He urges that recruiters, particularly, do a more responsible job by judging a man on his demonstrated or potential ability, not on his race.

He believes the following characteristics have been most important in his own career:

1. The ability to ignore the racial bias that he has encountered.
2. Good written and oral communication.
3. The ability to get a job done.

He has exploited every position he has held for its educational value. He hopes to continue to be involved in data processing at a managerial level; if that proves a dead end, he has some ideas, also, about pursuing a career in law.

"The constraints of discrimination in housing, employment, and public education confront most Negro professionals," he says. Yet he acknowledges that "the present phenomenon known as the data-processing marketplace" mitigates the employment constraint. Being a relatively new profession, data processing is free from some of the traditional biases against hiring minority-group members.

Arthur L. Hardeman

Here's how Arthur Hardeman replied when asked what characteristics seem essential to the Negro manager or professional.

1. He must be a good conversationalist and have ability in public relations (especially if he has whites reporting to him).
2. Decision making is necessary but must be coupled with a creative mind.
3. Clear and logical thinking is a must.
4. He must be pleasant to look at. "I'm convinced," Hardeman says, "that a good-looking black has a better chance at managerial success than an ugly one."
5. He must be impartial with respect to "brothers" working for him. "Hard to do!" Hardeman admits.

He points out that the first three qualities are essential regardless of race. But Nos. 4 and 5 seem particularly necessary for a minority-group member. Hardeman elaborates by pointing to two problems he faces in business that he believes do not confront most whites in the white-collar ranks: The first is the necessity to excel to be accepted even as an ordinary staff member. The second lies in the emotional area—the need to restrain one's emotions when discussing explosive topics such as riots or poverty.

Hardeman finds the second problem a perennial challenge, but he has resolved the first. He does excel as a computer programmer and systems analyst with the Sandia Corporation in Albuquerque, New Mexico.

Hardeman was born in 1944, in San Antonio, Texas. Although his mother earned little as a maid, she saw him through high school there. A four-year scholarship from the Field Foundation, supplemented by financial aid from the Kingmen's Social Club of San Antonio, saw him through four years at Morehouse College in Atlanta,

Georgia, where he received a bachelor's degree in mathematics in 1965.

A Sandia recruiter persuaded him to return to his native Southwest. Since his employment in 1965, he has been attending the University of New Mexico part time, working toward a master's degree in computer science.

Hardeman believes that education is one of the major keys to career advancement for minority-group members. For example, "Sandia is quite degree-conscious," says Hardeman, "and minority groups around this area are only recently becoming concerned about advanced education, although experience abounds." He rates personality and ambition next in importance. He also believes that every person, regardless of race, must rely primarily on himself for advancement. "Promotions are usually the result of outstanding performance."

His advice to other Negroes who wish to join the white-collar ranks: "Speak good English. Learn how important personal appearances can be. Talk to recruiters on campuses, visit personnel offices at companies you're interested in. Become adept at selling yourself. Send résumés widely."

Although he is the only Negro currently in his office, Hardeman is not worried about becoming a "showcase white-collar Negro" because he believes that his job has significance. However, he knows "brothers" who wrestle with this problem.

Other suggestions to the office aspirant: "Learn to participate freely in all office activity. Never take advantage of preferential treatment. Through experience, acquire a bit of professional pride and responsibility."

Hardeman is still a bachelor and young. He's ready to go anywhere that will advance his career.

Charles F. James

Chuck James has been a leader ever since his high school days. He was elected class president in his sophomore, junior, and senior years at Benjamin Franklin High School in Rochester, New York. He was vice-president of the student body in his junior year and captain of the football team as a senior.

At Cornell University, where he received an A.B. in sociology in 1957, he was secretary-treasurer of his freshman class and president of the sophomore class, and he won numerous awards. He financed his college education through a Cornell national scholarship, a Cornell state scholarship, a New York State cash scholarship, summer work as a truck driver, and part-time work during the school year as a cook's helper in a fraternity house.

He served in the Army from 1957 to 1962, emerging as a captain. He was stationed in Germany and had experience as a company commander and temporarily as a battalion commander. While attending the Army Language School in Monterey, California, to learn Arabic, he earned a private pilot's license.

James resigned from the Army to attend law school at Howard University, where he ranked first in his class for two years. He was class president in the second year. A scholarship and graduate fellowship helped finance his law education. He left Howard to join the New York Telephone Company as a management trainee but attended the Evening Division of New York University's School of Law to complete requirements for his doctor of law degree (J.D.) in 1966. A portion of his expenses at NYU was reimbursed by the tuition-aid plan of the New York Telephone Company.

At New York Telephone, Chuck James advanced rapidly—from manager of two long-distance and local-assistance telephone offices to manager of two information offices to staff supervisor, Operating

Staff—Traffic, and then in January 1969 to district traffic superintendent, responsible for the Manhattan Number Services District.

He aims still higher—to a vice-presidency, or more, with some major company. But he does *not* want a job in urban affairs. His principal problem in the business world which does not confront most whites is "to convince people that I have been chosen for a particular job because of my ability to get results rather than because I am black." Among the major characteristics essential to the Negro manager or professional he includes objectivity, the ability to see past color, a strong desire to succeed, impartiality, the ability to counsel and inspire others, a willingness to make decisions, and perseverance. He hastens to add that such characteristics are needed by any manager or professional, white or black.

All of Chuck James's associates at his level in New York Telephone are white, and he has no problems getting along with them. "I have experienced no difficulty in dealing with subordinates of either race," he comments, "but a few have had to be set straight initially. However, it was no problem."

He believes that white managers can help Negroes achieve white-collar promotions "by judging blacks by the same criteria they use to judge whites and by encouraging blacks who they think possess management potential." Like most blacks, Chuck James strongly contends that present managers should treat Negro white-collar employees no differently from any other employees. "All should be held to the same standards," he says, "and receive the same rewards."

In his opinion, blacks can best prepare themselves for the office environment "by getting out of all-black environments and learning the technical and social skills expected in the business world." He advises youngsters with white-collar aspirations as follows: "Where possible, attend integrated schools—elementary, high school, and college —so that you can gain a decent education and, more importantly, learn that whites are just people with whom you should not be afraid to compete."

Once a Negro has a white-collar job, James urges, he should "take advantage of company courses. Don't shy away from tough jobs or situations where you may have to 'push' others." As a manager, the black performs best "by demanding high performance from subordinates. When necessary, be tough in reprimanding or dismissing poor performers." But the most important test for a black person in a managerial or professional job, according to Chuck James, is this: "Do not overreact to real or supposed racial slights. React only to the extent appropriate to insure that the real slight will not be repeated."

Charles F. James was born in Rochester in 1935. His father is a shipping-receiving clerk for a wholesale produce firm in Rochester, and his mother is a housewife. James belongs to a number of organizations, including the Urban League of Essex County (N.J.), of which he is first vice-president; the Vice President's Task Force on Youth Motivation, Plans for Progress; the New York City Task Force, for which he was associate coordinator in 1967–1968; and the National Defense Executive Reserve.

He and his wife, the former Jean Hunter of Woodlawn, Ohio (Howard, 1958), are parents of an infant daughter, born in April 1969. Chuck continues with a program of self-education and improvement, which eventually will include study to pass the New Jersey Bar Examination. A commuter to New York City, Chuck James lives with his family in Millburn, New Jersey.

Robert Jenkins

Bob Jenkins wants an end to the double standard applied to whites and blacks in business and industry. "As a black man," he says, "I feel we are constantly on a proving ground. Work performance is scrutinized more for blacks than for whites. Unless you are a superstar, it takes you longer to make the grade." He advises Negroes in white-collar positions to "make management (or the union) aware of your dislike for double standards." The solution, Jenkins believes, is the straightforward one: "Drop double standards. If management hires a Negro for a given job, it must judge him—and reward him—on the basis of his performance, not his color."

Bob is a systems and procedures analyst with the Northern Illinois Gas Company in Aurora, Illinois. He gathers and analyzes facts in order to develop recommendations, write instructions, and gain acceptance for procedure projects. In these tasks, he needs to practice the art of persuasion, because most of his recommendations involve change and people often resist change. But he points out, "I find it no more difficult to deal with white associates than with Negroes in my company. My problem is not race here. It's human nature."

He acknowledges that he has to remind himself of that fact periodically. "I have to guard against seeing the race question in all my business activities," Jenkins says. "A black man can drift into double standards, too." For that reason, he places self-control high on the list of characteristics essential to the Negro manager or professional. He also considers fairness and justness top qualities needed by blacks in white-collar jobs.

He advises Negroes who aspire to white-collar jobs: "Learn as much about the business as you can. Learn to get along with people and their attitudes."

Bob Jenkins believes business should go beyond conventional recruiting—college visits, the use of employment agencies, advertising, and the like—to find black people for white-collar positions. "Recruit also at the high school level. By going there, we may be able to find talent in people who can't afford to go to college or who aren't motivated to do so. If we can instill in them a desire for higher education or find a way to help them get it, we may be recruiting for the future."

Jenkins is working for his own future. He already has his B.B.A. in marketing from Fairfield University in Fairfield, Connecticut, but is also working at night toward a master's degree in marketing and personnel. Besides his academic prowess, he excels in sports: he was captain of Fairfield's basketball team and also played intramural softball.

His career has included a season as freshman basketball coach at Fairfield; a three-year stint at the Lycoming Division of Avco, where he was a procedures and value analyst in Stratford, Connecticut; and a year selling life insurance for Equitable. He joined Northern Illinois in 1966, first as a sales representative. He was promoted to his present assignment in 1968.

Jenkins was born in New York City in 1939. He is an ardent hobbyist in arts and crafts, bowling, photography, and gardening and has served as an arts and crafts instructor for the Catholic Youth Organization in New York. Other sidelines have included sports refereeing and umpiring and service as an oxygen therapist in hospitals in Bridgeport and the Chicago area.

He has a wife and five children—two sons and three daughters.

Alex J. Murray

"With each new person you meet—black or white—you have to convince him anew that you are in charge and give the orders." So says Alex J. Murray, commenting about the special problems that a black manager faces which do not normally confront the white manager. "A white manager is almost automatically accepted," he believes.

He solves the problem by "letting the person know who's boss in a firm but pleasant way. I take charge of the things that are my responsibility."

Alex Murray is currently responsible for special employment training as a program coordinator for the St. Regis Paper Company in Pittsburgh. He believes he has found his field—personnel and industrial relations—after trying a variety of others first. He has been a health investigator, schoolteacher, and analytical chemist and has made a variety of minor investigations of still other job areas. Yet he doesn't regret his extensive sampling of many employment possibilities—it's good background for employee relations.

Alex Murray is continuing his graduate education in the field of analytical chemistry and is now writing his master's thesis; he has taken all the necessary courses at Duquesne University. He received his B.S. from California State College.

He says that the characteristic most essential to the Negro manager or professional is the ability "to communicate his ideas. He must also be able to evaluate a problem or situation and deal with it effectively in spite of difficulties that may arise because of his color," he explains.

"When I was placed in charge of the spectographic department at my last job, I managed an operation which consisted of one foreman and several employees—all white. This situation would have been difficult had I not decided that I would show all these people that I could do the job best. When I had proved it, I found that I had overcome whatever handicap my color may have caused, and I had also built up a lot of respect for me privately."

From his experience in employment training, Alex Murray draws two major conclusions: First, many black people have the potential for managerial and professional work. But, second, most of the people with the potential do not have the experience. Formal managerial or professional education poses less of a problem than experience, although education, too, is essential. The challenge lies in somehow giving blacks on-the-job time in managerial or professional work. Murray's suggestions for doing this are as follows:

1. Make sure that black people have responsibility, even at the lower or entry-level jobs.
2. Do not shelter black people; expect them to do a job and make mistakes.

Alex Murray sees no special problems in identifying Negroes with managerial or professional capabilities. "You do it the same way you identify whites with such potential." Most such people identify themselves, he believes. He has little patience with anyone who just sits waiting to be tapped. "Seek out opportunity," he advises. "Don't expect it to come looking for you."

Because he has observed numerous Negroes in professional and managerial positions, Murray's analysis of their performance merits attention. "A black man (or woman) should understand that he's not the only one in that office who has problems. Be sensitive to that fact." He points out that some Negroes limit their effectiveness as managers or professionals by being insensitive to the likelihood that their white colleagues have difficulties, too. "Their obstacles may be different from a black man's" he says, "but they probably exist."

On the other side of the coin, the white manager or professional should sharpen his perception of the Negro's typical problems in an office environment—possibly less experience than white colleagues possess, an uneasiness in communicating in terms familiar to whites, and a general unsureness that may be masked by belligerence, apathy, or a blankness often mistaken for indifference or even stupidity.

Alex Murray was born on April 20, 1934, in Elizabeth, Pennsylvania. His father is a steelworker. He and his wife have one young daughter.

Theodore Nims, Jr.

"Some Negroes are putting too much emphasis on being identified as black rather than being recognized as leaders or authorities in particular fields," believes Ted Nims, district representative for General Electric's Housewares Division in the Cleveland (Ohio) Region. He's responsible for the sales and marketing of GE clocks and personal-care and floor-care products in part of Ohio, western Pennsylvania, and western New York.

"It isn't necessary for us to wear Afro dress to be identified as black," he comments. "Wear such styles if you like them, but for no other reason. The whites already know that we're black. Added emphasis on our race, I've noticed, tends to make whites think of us even more as members of a group, not as individuals. If we continue to perform well on those jobs previously closed to us, the whites will really recognize us as individuals. I don't think I'm betraying my race if I prefer to be known as Ted Nims, top salesman, rather than as Ted Nims, Negro."

Nims points out that there are many openings in sales and marketing for blacks. "However, the average Negro college student still doesn't picture blacks in such a field with major corporations, because there are still so few of us employed in this work. It is up to individuals who are successful to relate back to the college students. We also have to persuade our Negro colleges to begin putting more emphasis on courses relating to business."

He urges students and instructors to learn more about business by seeking summer employment in industry and by taking field trips. Since 1966, Ted has been a board member with Jobs Clearing House, Inc., an organization based in Boston and dedicated to convincing young college graduates to seek jobs in industry. He has visited several Negro colleges on recruiting trips. In April 1968, he was a consultant to a business conference at Texas Southern University. Representatives, who were present from most of the Negro colleges, were interested in receiving recommendations from Negro college graduates in industry on how they can better prepare their students for entering big business.

Nims was graduated from Florida A & M University, Tallahassee, in 1964 with a B.S. in business administration. He was born in Tallahassee in 1942. His mother, a beautician, moved north when he was young, and he got his public schooling mostly in New York and Connecticut, graduating from a Bridgeport high school in 1960.

Nims discovered his bent for selling when he got a job with a major discount department-store chain in Bridgeport while he was still only a junior in high school. He progressed rapidly from stock boy to assistant housewares manager. He learned something of the manufacturing side of housewares by working one summer between college years making fans in GE's Bridgeport plant.

When he had finished college, he sought a marketing job with his summer employer, GE. He went after a position at the manufacturer's level rather than at the retail level because opportunities and salaries seemed higher. He became a sales trainee for GE Housewares in June 1964. After this course, he moved on to Boston as a sales specialist and district representative. He was soon promoted to district representative and office manager at the Syracuse, New York, office. From there, he progressed to his current job in Cleveland.

The large majority of his contacts are white. "In my initial meeting with them," he comments, "some are overly cautious with me, as though they fear that they'll do or say something wrong that will be offensive. In my business dealings in the white world, I don't see much of the old-style hostility that was supposed to have made it impossible for a black to sell to whites." He elaborates: "With a white contact, I often find that I have to put him at ease—not the other way round. I try to do this by getting it across that I am only another man with a job to do, just like him."

Ted Nims believes that the characteristics which lead to success in business—dependability, honesty, persuasiveness, perseverance, and ambition—are the same whether a man is black or white, "except that Negroes have to make them more obvious than whites do—sell them harder, in other words."

More than ever, Nims is convinced that marketing is his forte, and he intends to stay in it. He hopes to be responsible for making sales and marketing plans on a national basis in the not-too-distant future, "resulting, in the years to come, in a possible top sales and marketing position." He intends to go to evening college eventually to get his master's degree, and he will also take advantage of some of the many courses offered by General Electric.

Ted Nims and his wife, Gloria, are the parents of two girls, born in 1966 and 1969.

He says: "Looking to the future, I would advise a youngster about to choose a career to enter business if he or she had the characteristics to be successful. I believe he will have it easier than I and other Negroes of today have had it, because whites will consider him first for ability to perform and only second as a Negro."

O. S. Williams, Jr.

A person with a high degree of expertise, especially in technical areas, can find a good job and win promotions regardless of race. That is the lesson to be learned from the career of O. S. (Ozzie) Williams, Jr. He is now manager of spacecraft development for the Grumman Aerospace Corporation in Bethpage, New York. His responsibilities include marketing, contract negotiations, long-range technical planning, proposal coordination, and customer relations, all in the area of post-Apollo space exploration.

The bulk of Williams's 27 years as an aeronautical/aerospace engineer has been devoted to research and development, with emphasis on rocket engines since 1956. Before joining Grumman, Williams was a senior project engineer in the Reaction Motors Division of Thiokol Chemical Corporation, where he was instrumental in demonstrating the feasibility of rapidly pulsed rocket engines for spacecraft control. He presented the results of this work in two technical papers published by the American Rocket Society.

Before entering the rocket industry, Williams was on the research and development staff of Greer Hydraulics, Inc., and was responsible for developing the first successful airborne radio beacon for locating crashed aircraft. Earlier, during World War II, he worked for the Republic Aviation Corporation, first as an armament designer on the P-47 fighter, later as an aerodynamicist on high-performance jet aircraft and experimental missiles.

He joined Grumman in 1961, where for six years he was assigned to the Apollo Lunar Module (LM) Project as manager of reaction control. He was responsible for design and development of the rocket system with which the Apollo astronauts controlled the LM spacecraft during its lunar mission. In addition to direct supervision of an engineering task force at Grumman, the assignment included technical and cost management of more than $30 million worth of subcontracts for reaction-control hardware. This involved such specialized technologies as bipropellant rocket engines, thermodynamics, electronics, metallurgy, hydraulics, and pneumatics.

Williams's primary and secondary education in Brooklyn public schools was followed by attendance at New York University from 1938 to 1942; he received a bachelor's degree in aeronautical engineering. Subsequent graduate studies led to a master's degree in aeronautical engineering in 1947.

He reached his present job as manager of spacecraft development partly as a result of pressure by black employees on Grumman management. Williams has been involved in helping black employees there secure better jobs and persuading the company to foster upward mobility for members of minorities. As cofounder of the Big Brother Organization in Grumman, devoted to self-help by and for black employees, he believes white managers can best help black people achieve promotions "by steering them into key assignments and encouraging maximum effort, and by preparing other whites to accept earned promotions on the part of blacks."

He believes black people can best prepare themselves as professionals by getting a solid educational background, with advanced study, if possible, and by taking advantage of company-sponsored training programs. To qualify as a potential manager, he feels, you must also—

1. Volunteer for tough, competitive assignments on the job.
2. Constantly seek increasing responsibility.
3. Recognize the fact that success for most whites is the result of ability and hard work. Be prepared to work even harder for your own success.
4. Develop empathy for fellow workers without reducing your own competitive drive.

Williams also thinks that Negroes can prepare themselves for the office environment in clerical and comparable positions by following these precepts:

1. Attend high school and college "career days," especially those which feature black representatives from business and industry.
2. Emphasize language-skill subjects in school.
3. Participate in office-oriented workshop sessions in schools, churches, the YMCA, and so on.

He believes blacks who have "made it" in the business world should accept the responsibility of aiding others of their race to match their performance. "Their personal encouragement should help," he says. "At the very least, successful black employees should supplement the efforts of recruitment specialists." In addition, programs are needed in which such employees can directly assist and motivate other blacks toward success within the corporate structure. Such a program is being implemented at Grumman by the Big Brother Organization, which, as has been noted, is a group of black volunteers devoted to job advancement and training for, and individual self-improvement by, black employees. Williams especially urges that black people get challenging assignments. He believes that the black man or woman who aspires to a managerial or professional job "must develop deep understanding of white subordinates and superiors and expect little understanding in return."

Williams was born in Washington, D.C., in 1921 but has lived in New York since he was five. He is married and is the father of three children, of whom one is working toward a Ph.D. in psychology at the University of Pittsburgh and another is an engineering student at Princeton University. Mrs. Williams is a teacher of retarded children in the New York City public schools. In addition to science and engineering, Williams's interests include sculpture, creative writing, photography, bowling, and fishing, and he shares with his oldest son a growing enthusiasm for sailplane flying.

DISCUSSION

"Potential black members of the white-collar ranks must have as their goal the acquisition of some type of formal training. Without it, the black man leaves himself more open to continued rejection." It was William Outlaw who said that, but he reflects the opinion of every Negro manager and professional interviewed. They all show a formidable thirst for knowledge. John Walker took a job with the Chemical Bank, New York, largely because he could enter its training program. James Walton urges fellow blacks to "take advantage of the special seminars and courses offered through many companies . . . and to keep up on business reading."

General Electric tells its new people: "It is important to recognize as you begin a career . . . that virtually continuous education will be necessary to maintain your proficiency and assure continuing advancement. Technology once progressed at a rate which made it possible for a man to learn for a while and then apply that learning for a long time without falling too far behind. Not so any more. Today the time lapse between the birth of a scientific idea and its practical application has become so short that an employee simply must merge continuing education with his working career."

Blacks, then, have a dual impetus toward education: the substandard educational background from which many of them suffer, and the acceleration of knowledge, especially in technological and managerial areas.

Special Educational Cases

Do black people resent the fact that they may need special educational aid? They may resent it, but still they recognize it—and most of those interviewed want to do something about it. They think of training courses as entrance ramps onto superhighways, serving to let one build up speed and meet the normal flow of traffic.

Many of those interviewed agreed with Roosevelt Powell, who said: "Black people come from different environments and cannot be expected to perform as whites do in a white society." Different treatment for blacks should include, Powell believes, extended training to insure indoctrination even in such basics as the "language" of the office, which is completely unfamiliar to many Negroes (and possibly also to whites) going into entry-level jobs. He gives, as examples of unfamiliar office vocabulary, "the cycle" (accounting period) and "a snap of core" (a printout of computer storage).

Alex Murray, who is responsible for special training employment at the St. Regis Paper Company, notes that when special training is needed, it should be offered in a way that does not shelter black people.

Nate King sees supplemental training as almost a therapeutic service, to give white-collar aspirants "the necessary confidence to perform the jobs." He points out that many don't even have rudimentary clerical skills, which are necessary in most white-collar positions. He advises: "Know your way around a typewriter and a file drawer, and know the elementary clerical procedures." But he admits that this knowledge may be difficult to acquire in many of the substandard ghetto schools.

Techniques of Teaching

Many companies offer formal training in clerical work and other lower-level white-collar work. The Emerson Electric Company, of St. Louis, for example, uses closed-circuit television to show clerical trainees their job operations in slow motion. Hoffman-La Roche, Inc. also uses audiovisual aids to train clerks in its Newark, New Jersey, offices. The McGraw-Hill Book Company, part of McGraw-Hill, Inc., New York, has an extensive program to teach business math, English, typewriting skills, and other subjects. And these are only a few of many possible examples. Most teaching for the higher white-collar echelons emphasizes on-the-job, individual treatment. Oral and on-the-spot visual communication has proved the most practical means of training. Basically, the procedure is to explain the job, then show it, then let the employee try it—a "talk and show" proposition. Instead of on-the-job techniques, however, many companies provide a basic training school for new supervisors.

In some cases, many of the following suggestions can and should be used for potential managers and professionals.

1. *Begin with what the Negro already knows.* This establishes confidence and reduces nervousness. Refer to related experience. Draw parallels.

One white manager gave this advice to a young black supervisor who experienced difficulties with his people—white and black—during his first days as boss: "I don't think this trouble has a thing to do with race. It's more as if you're a new boy at school. Remember how the kids had to try you out? Test you? That's what these people are doing. Take the tests calmly, but meet them. You won't have to fight the biggest kid in the class, as at school, but you'll have to pass some kind of test to their satisfaction. Show them you know the job. Prove you don't wilt under pressure."

2. *Go ahead bit by bit.* Divide the training into manageable segments and do it a step at a time. The manager we quoted above took the first thing first—the employees' "testing" of the new supervisor's mettle. He left until later some of the more subtle aspects of supervision—appraisal of workers to determine who does what best, for example, and keeping competitive instincts in a delicate balance that stimulates people to do their best without promoting divisive rivalries.

3. *Repeat.* But avoid boredom by repeating in different ways. The manager in the example used here wanted his new supervisor to motivate the employees more than his predecessor had. But he was careful not to overuse the word "motivate." He used synonyms—challenge, impel, incite, stimulate—in discussing the subject. At appropriate moments, he would drop comments to the supervisor—"I think Ed would do better if you could find something about his work to praise. Overdo it a little; it won't hurt. He's got an underdeveloped ego." Or, "Give those special jobs to Fred occasionally. It will keep Charley from thinking he's teacher's pet."

4. *Practice,* to make as perfect as possible. Although this is not a normal training technique, the manager insisted that the supervisor report to him every few days on what he had done to motivate those who worked for him. The manager was doing more than checking; he was insisting that the supervisor practice stimulating his people. And this provided a handy way to appraise the new supervisor's techniques and to suggest additional ones. Incidentally, it also accomplished the "repetition" step.

5. *Stimulate questions.* The reporting process just described served to bring out the supervisor's questions. Why does one approach to motivation work one day and not the next, or on some people but not others? What approaches alienate people? Why?

6. *Try to be positive and encouraging.* All people respond best to encouragement, but especially blacks, most of whom have seen more than their share of life's negative side. The manager looked for things to praise in the new supervisor's handling of his job and he lauded them fulsomely. Another point: Praise in public, but censure in private.

7. *Use visual aids when practical.* People are used to learning by both aural and visual means, but they learn more readily by visual means in this age of television and films. This applies particularly to young black people. Visual techniques are important in another way, too: Most people learn more readily when they are shown than when they are told.

For example, the manager found it helpful to have the new supervisor stay at his elbow for a few hours a week during the initial period on his unfamiliar job. "See how I handled Ed?" he would say after a session with one employee. "I tried to build him up." Or the manager would point out the fact that two employees in the supervisor's group seemed to be particularly good friends. "Notice how they seem to stimulate each other?" he would ask. "I wonder how they would do as a team on the Smith job? It needs two people."

8. *Show the individual where he belongs in the scene.* The manager carefully demonstrated where the supervisor fit into the entire operation, emphasizing his importance to the success of the whole. The manager gave a history of the supervisor's job and thumbnail sketches of some predecessors, putting the supervisor in as favorable a light as possible.

9. *Show where the work being done fits in.* For example, the

manager gave the history of the work, told why it was done in a certain way, and told why it was needed.

10. *Put the new man on his own at the proper time.* Sooner or later all of us have to walk for the first time. The manager who gave the "at my elbow" sessions abandoned them when the supervisor began to anticipate his points and comments and started to show polite impatience with his explanations. "I probably waited too long," said the manager. Many teachers do.

11. *Follow through.* The manager unobtrusively checked to see how the new supervisor was doing. Reporting sessions, which may be continued permanently, serve a useful function here. They can also be used to make corrections privately.

12. *Watch for the better "students."* This manager was impressed with the new supervisor during the instruction period and made a mental note to keep an eye on him for further promotion. During training, you ordinarily maintain closer contact with the neophyte than at any other time. It may be well to keep a record of your impressions so that you can eventually recommend him for a likely assignment.

Teaching Attitudes

Techniques of instruction, however, prove much less important than attitude. The teacher can make a lasting impression—good, bad, or indifferent—on a black learning a managerial or professional job. As you teach him, ask yourself these questions, bearing in mind that you often are teaching your own job to a successor.

1. Do I believe in what I teach?
2. Do I regard the "student" as a member of a group or as an individual?
3. Am I presenting the material in a way I would like it presented to me?
4. Do I present it clearly and concisely?
5. Have I shown patience?
6. Have I remained calm?
7. Have I shown enthusiasm for the job?
8. Have I encouraged the new man to higher performance?

9. Have I corrected mistakes tactfully but unmistakably?
10. Have I praised sincerely and generously?
11. Have I stimulated questions and comments?
12. Have I presented the *why*, in addition to the *what*, of the job?
13. Have I put across the standards of performance expected?
14. Have I made clear the rewards for a job well done?
15. Have I made clear that the job carries with it the freedom to fail, provided that the failure is because of ignorance or human error rather than willfulness or criminal carelessness?

The freedom to fail is important—especially to blacks, many of whom may be nervous, or at least uneasy, as they try to enter the white man's world of management and technology. If you convey to them such a grim idea of the consequences of failure that they freeze from fear of doing something wrong, your teaching has failed. When you instruct, put across the notion that you encourage the freedom to experiment and to take reasonable risks. Acknowledge that the odds are high that some experiments and risks won't work out.

Continuing with our example, in a reporting meeting, the new supervisor ruefully confessed to his manager that one of his motivational ideas had failed. He had made extensive changes in work assignments among his people, hoping for a better match between tasks and workers, but the experiment had gone hopelessly awry. The manager masked his irritation. "I agree with your analysis of the match-ups," he said. "I think the experiment went wrong because you made the changes too quickly. You get people upset by sudden change. Hold on to this idea, but make the changes gradually. And always explain in advance to the people involved what you're doing and why."

The supervisor tried his idea again six months later, but he made the changes much more gradually. The second time around, they worked out quite well.

When Teaching Fails

Some white supervisors may automatically attribute learning failures to the black students' shortcomings. Before you do that, look to your own techniques and attitudes. For instance, are you supposed to teach or explain the job? Did you hurry your instruction? If you violated one or more of the dozen teaching techniques or answered no to one or more of the 15 questions on attitude, the fault may lie more with you. If the answer does not seem to lie there, consider these factors:

1. *Have you chosen the right person for the job?* Mark Grant summed up a common problem in this area. We'll repeat his story here: "There was only one other Negro programmer on the floor. He was assigned as my mentor, presumably because it was thought that I would feel more comfortable with someone of the same skin pigmentation. The results were disastrous, as we were poles apart in personality, temperament, and work habits."

Remember that race is seldom very relevant to work assignments. Yet assignments are often made on that basis alone.

2. *Do you understand thoroughly what you teach?* In addition, make sure you fully understand the lingo of the job you are teaching. All companies and many departments use specialized language to represent whole concepts or practices. Be sure that you know such usages and pass them along.

3. *Have you timed your teaching correctly?* If a manager starts off with the more subtle motivational aspects of a new supervisor's job, he may lose him. Many teachers naturally tend to stress what interests them most, sometimes broaching it much too soon.

4. *Have you found a "peg," or reason, for teaching?* Some people, including blacks, may resent being taught. They may feel it smacks of patronage or condescension. The best teachers instruct so subtly that the learner scarcely realizes it. Our manager often achieved this in teaching his new supervisor.

5. *Have you appraised the counterinfluences in your teaching?* Racial prejudice—real or imagined—looms here. Oddly, the problem rarely results because a manager shows blatant prejudice or suffers so badly from "foot-in-mouth disease" that he inadvertently offends the learners. The real difficulty stems from overcaution—"as though they fear that they'll do or say something wrong that will be offensive," as Ted Nims puts it. "In my business dealings in the white world, I don't see much of the old-style hostility."

This walking-on-eggs attitude poses the most severe difficulty, the sharpest counterinfluence in teaching blacks. The best teaching environment results when a free-and-easy relationship exists between teacher and student. It sometimes proves difficult to achieve when a white tries to teach a black; but if you experience difficulties in this regard, here's a suggestion—don't try to teach in the conventional sense; instead, explain the requirements and let the learner commit his own mistakes, making it clear that he has the freedom to fail the first few times he is on his own.

Postmortem on Postmortems

The postmortem session is so common a teaching device that it merits special mention. When the manager of our example set up reporting periods, they often turned out to be postmortems. The negative potential of such sessions may be minimized by—

1. *Keeping matters impersonal.* Remain unemotional; don't assign blame, and don't criticize.

2. *Analyzing why and how a mistake was made.* Enter into this in a spirit of dispassionate inquiry. Always emphasize why it's necessary to know the reasons for errors.

3. *Accenting the positive.* Point out that we all learn more from our mistakes than from our successes. For example, in the new-assignment fiasco just described, the manager indicated that such mishaps had occurred before. He emphasized that his objective was to find ways of preventing it from happening again.

4. *Asking for suggestions on how to prevent similar occurrences.* Give the supervisor time to think of alternatives.

5. *Trying out the suggestions on a test basis.* The manager advised the supervisor to try the match-up idea again six months later, but with important differences. The supervisor, you'll remember, instituted the changes gradually the second time, and he let the people involved know exactly what he was doing and why.

6. *Canvassing the opinions of others.* Suggest to the supervisor that he check his peers to learn if they have had similar experiences.

7. *Putting a report in writing on the solution to a problem.* The manager in our example insisted that the supervisor do this to crystallize the solution he had in mind. After the assignment fiasco, for example, the manager's regular reporting sessions insured that postmortems occurred promptly. Speed, he knew, is essential to the effec-

tiveness of the postmortem. The manager arranged for the supervisor to do most of the work in the sessions himself, because the "do it yourself" aspect of the postmortem is important in the learning process.

The manager we've been discussing was especially pleased that the supervisor volunteered the news about his reassignment troubles: Self-appraisal is the best kind of postmortem.

The Refresher Course

A manager can use reporting sessions for still another purpose—to provide a refresher course. The first difficulty with refreshers lies in knowing when you need them. Some of the signs are a productivity slump, a quality dip, a rise in absenteeism, and a general staleness.

The next difficulty with refreshers lies in putting the teaching into new contexts and new words—creating a changed approach. People often resist refreshers because they expect boring repetition, and a refresher implies (sometimes correctly) that they have not been performing up to par.

A manager can overcome some of these problems by—

1. *Regularizing the procedure for supplemental training.* Reporting periods can accomplish this.

2. *Telling why the refresher is needed.* One manager acknowledged frankly that he wanted continual refreshers because this was the best way to learn.

3. *Emphasizing the need to do the job even better.* The manager can note past improvements but also should cite competitive and other factors to show that even more improvement is necessary.

4. *Keeping notes on former teaching approaches,* so that methods can be varied the next time around. After each reporting session, a manager should make brief notes on what has been covered and what was said. When ideas occur to him, he can note alternative ways to handle a problem the next time.

5. *Using the refresher as a means of critical reappraisal.* The manager should make the refresher do double duty. He should stimulate the asking of such questions as these: "Is the way I've been doing the job the best way?" "What other methods are possible?" "What can

I do to win more support and improve *esprit de corps* among my people?"

Principles of Persuasion

That last question highlights a continuing concern for most Negroes who hold or aspire to managerial positions. It also frequently impinges on the consciousness of black professionals—though not as often as for managers.

Art White, the Anheuser-Busch distributor, underscores this concern when he advises: "Explain the incentives available for a job well done, for this is what motivates men." Robert Jenkins puts it in somewhat different terms: "Learn to get along with people and their attitudes." Alex Flamer. has something of this in mind when he advises: "Be sociable." Chuck James says the same thing: "Learn social skills expected in the business world."

All this boils down to persuasion—getting colleagues, white and black, to do what you want them to do. The following nine principles of persuasion may help whites and blacks alike to influence each other more effectively.

1. *It is important to state conclusions.* You must make crystal-clear where you stand and why you take such a position. The facts alone won't persuade. Others may not draw the same conclusion as you from the facts, because their perceptions may be quite different. But your conclusions must be logical and responsive to a need.

2. *Emotions persuade more effectively than facts, especially for the short pull.* Of course, facts must lie at the foundation of your emotion, but you need an emotional catalyst to put them across. Facts come across best when you can idealize them. For example, the manager who got involved in the reassignment problem, in putting across to the new supervisor the benefits of motivating people, idealized the results.

3. *Time proves a key factor in persuasion.* Even intelligent people have trouble grasping new ideas immediately. So don't expect to sell new notions quickly. Take your time. Don't rush.

4. *Objections are almost certain to arise.* These must be anticipated. When you try to persuade people, you seek to change their ways, which is usually a distasteful business.

5. *Resistance is to be expected—invariably.* Don't, therefore, be upset by it. Many managers lose the persuasion battle because they get exasperated by resistance and show their annoyance. As a result, people get their backs up even higher. Resistance comes in many forms. Black people are experts at expressing it in hundreds of subtle ways, because they have had a couple of centuries of experience in doing so.

6. *Positive personal involvement is the goal.* This sixth principle often proves one of the best ways to make people want to do as you want. Show that it's in their own enlightened self-interest to do things in a different way. One manager persuaded his new supervisor to concentrate on motivation, even though this is a difficult and often intangible concept, because he showed what benefits could come to the supervisor—in higher productivity and the advancement of his own career.

7. *It must be made clear that the desired action is possible.* A manager may be able, for instance, to point to other supervisors who have motivated their crews to higher productivity.

8. *Motives should be stated frankly.* A manager has a vested interest in pushing motivation. The better his supervisors do, the better he is performing. When you don't mention such obvious motives, you unwittingly impart dubiety to your objectives. Of course you have your own interests in mind—what's wrong with saying so?

9. *Credibility must be guarded.* A reputation for personal honesty is hard to build but easy to demolish—one false step usually suffices. You can never persuade effectively, without credibility, no matter how skillfully you follow the other eight principles. Credibility, then, must be the main weapon in your arsenal of persuasion.

Super Supervision

Fundamental to all good training is the instructor. Dick Lawson puts it this way: "Learn about your boss and his job." The recognition that the boss can make or break instruction is implicit here. The following ten good supervisory practices (some of them have already been alluded to) are of special significance in training young Negroes:

1. *Praise publicly, censure privately.* Accustomed as they have been to two centuries of public censure, blacks particularly will welcome this.

2. *Give credit when and where due.* All people want this. Give it quickly, with sincerity.

3. *Explain the reason for change, and announce change well in advance.* Although the instructor should vary his *methods* of instruction, he should not change his *concepts* of instruction without explaining how and why he is doing so. For example, when the manager who abandoned the "at my elbow" concept did so, he first announced that he would do it the following week, and he explained the change with a compliment—that the supervisor no longer needed these sessions.

4. *Let people know how they're doing.* Uneasy in the white-collar world, blacks especially want to know where they stand.

5. *Make the best use of individual ability.* The Negro has not often experienced this luxury during his life, and he will respond to such treatment like a match to flame.

6. *Delegate responsibility.* And let the black person carry the ball in his own way. Supervise, but don't "snoopervise."

7. *Be considerate.* Give sincere attention to a Negro's feelings, desires, suggestions, and questions.

8. *Lead, don't drive.* You can lead much more easily than you can drive. Why try to drive, then, especially when results nearly always prove much better under good leadership than under "driver-ship"?

9. *Listen to black people.* As we will learn in the chapter on communication, listening requires skill under even the best circumstances. As a result of a kind of subliminal effect of racial prejudice, whites may not listen effectively to blacks. Make a concentrated effort to approach their questions and troubles with sympathy and understanding. Hear their complaints and suggestions.

10. *Know black people.* Dick Lawson implies this when he urges white managers to "make the time to teach us."

Priming the Pump

Many white young adults who enter the job market to become potential managers or professionals are already partly trained. Their parents are managers and professionals, so the children have absorbed some of the mores, lore, and background of white-collar positions almost since birth. As youngsters, they have frequently held part-time jobs of the white-collar type, where they have been able to pick up more background.

Not so with the typical black entrant into the white-collar job field. The odds are that neither of his parents ever held a managerial or professional job in business or industry. His part-time work may have been in menial positions.

Although this situation is changing, many blacks still start from a lower point of knowledge than their white counterparts when they take entry-level positions in the managerial and professional ranks. For this reason, the employer may need to prime the pump more carefully with a black candidate than with a white one—at least for the present.

It is probably no accident that blacks are doing relatively better in white-collar positions in newer industries, because new techniques and technologies are involved. Whites had less of a head start in computer work and similar areas than in more established fields. Moreover, the demand for talent in the new fields is so great that employers stop looking at color and begin seeking ability only.

The phenomenon has occurred before. Jewish immigrants dominated the early days of the motion-picture industry because it was a new field where they had fewer job disadvantages than in older businesses. German immigrants dominated the infant American dye and chemical industries before and after World War I for much the same reason.

Strictly speaking, we can't say that Negroes today are immigrants in this country, but in a sense they are immigrants in the white-collar job market because of their late entry into the economic mainstream.

Rising Tide of Education

The training that employers offer to young black aspirants for white-collar jobs necessarily comes after much of the formal education that these blacks receive before entering the business world.

Harvey Brewster urges the youngster to start early to pursue a professional or managerial career. "Explore the various jobs in a particular field of interest before the junior year in high school," he advises. John Chadwell, an educator-turned-businessman, says: "Get a good liberal education and then develop a specialty." Pierre Dillard recommends the cooperative approach to education—a period in school alternating with a period on a job—as a good way to become acclimatized to professional work. Bernard Walker, whose job is to provide management training at the Carnation Company's Houston Fresh Milk and Ice Cream Division, urges blacks to take advantage of company-sponsored courses and tuition-refund programs. O. S. Williams seconds the point about the need for continuing academic work even after a job has been won; he also suggests emphasis on language-skill subjects in school.

Jim White, manager of educational relations for Honeywell, sums it up: "Take more courses in business administration and psychology in college, participate in in-service management courses, get exposure to as much business experience as possible, and keep everlastingly at the process of education, both on the job and in formal courses in universities."

The managers and professionals interviewed recognize that members of their race must ride with the rising tide of education on the American scene. As recently as the early 1950s, the United States was spending on education an amount equal to about 3 percent of the gross national product. Today that percentage has more than doubled, and so has the GNP.

By 1975, the percentage should climb still higher. We should anticipate an increasing proportion of students—white and black—completing high school and going on to college, a great growth of junior colleges, still higher public and private expenditures for education because of higher salary schedules, lower pupil-teacher ratios, and investments in computer-assisted instruction and other new materials and methods. By 1975 we shall probably have established a norm of 14 years of free education, with greatly expanded scholarship and loan funds to carry students beyond that to college. After this period of formal education, the process of learning and retraining will be expected to continue throughout a person's career.

Society places an increasing premium on more and better education, in recognition of the fact that change demands versatility and flexibility. These, in turn, demand even more education and a continuing flow of new knowledge. Education and knowledge, of course, have been important factors in society for centuries, but both the degree and the character of their importance are now changing fast. Education up until now has been largely concerned with the transmission of accumulated knowledge and the perpetuation of the culture; from now on, though, it may become more a process of developing skill in thought processes and in preparation for change. In the past, knowledge has consisted mainly of what has been termed "folk knowledge," practical information about observable and tangible phenomena. In the future, theoretical knowledge may become decisive for society.

This upgrading of the importance of education also results, in part, from a new way of looking at it: The period of formal schooling is increasingly being regarded as an "investment" rather than a "consumption." Also, education is now often viewed as a "revolutionary" force, especially by blacks. Their increasing education and their growing economic power are changing their self-image. The better-educated Negro has more self-respect. He wants to be treated more as an individual, he has less tolerance for organizational restraints, and he has different and higher expectations of what he wants to put into a job and what he wants to get out of it.

An Educational Parenthesis

Perhaps the most remarkable phenomenon of the late 1960s—remarkable both for its vehemence and for its universality—was the series of student revolts that hit countries as diverse and dispersed as Japan and France, Italy and Mexico, Pakistan and the United States. Although the precise nature and causes of the revolts varied from country to country, there were common elements—opposition to the Vietnam war, the idea that universities are undemocratic structures, and a feeling that the education offered lacks relevance.

In the United States, Negroes have played a prominent part in the student revolts—to such an extent, indeed, that some employers have looked askance at every black college graduate who seeks employment in industry. Yet the odds are strongly against the possibility that extremism and violence will be continued directly into the world of business.

First, Negro radicals aren't likely to be interested in white-collar jobs. Second, the militant element among students is small (estimates vary from 2 to 5 percent). After the initial successes of this element in gaining the support of a larger body for specific causes, it seems now to be on the brink of alienating this wider support because of its violence and lack of constructive alternatives. The strong probability is that, given any reasonable choice between reform and revolution, the great majority of even today's "concerned" college students will choose the former, although as time proceeds the reforming students will graduate and may see the need for reforms in industry.

The college revolt, in which Negroes have played a prominent part, is nevertheless changing education, and implications for the business world, especially concerning managerial and professional jobs, are already emerging.

For example, employers may be interviewing younger college graduates, including Negroes. A radical departure from the traditional "lock step" progress through the schools, and revision of the "grade-level expectations" which are so much a part of the present educational system, will develop. The bright young people whom business hopes to attract will probably have graduated earlier in life than the previous generation.

Also, "new math" and "new science" are precursors of much more widespread curriculum revisions that will work their way through the schools. Similar revisions are coming in engineering and business administration. If you think you have trouble understanding your youngster's math homework assignment, wait until you try grappling with business-administration concepts held by your new recruit—white or black—on the management training program.

Your new management or engineering recruit will be much more visually oriented than orally oriented—far more so than his predecessor of four or five years earlier—because much greater educational use will be made of visual materials (including educational television and closed-circuit television). He will be more accustomed to learning visually than to learning orally.

In addition, the new recruit will expect more individual counseling, because he will be experiencing more of it during his educational career, especially in such areas as career selection, college selection, and emotional problems. Vocational courses, too, will receive increased emphasis, with companies participating more in the structuring—and even in the conducting—of these courses.

However, despite the potential for improvement in the educational system represented by these probabilities, a relative decline in the quality of education is still a threat. The growing demand for college-level education may cause a diffusion in the supply of competent teachers. Also, there may be a temptation to lower degree qualifications in an effort to meet the increasing need for graduates.

In summary, as an employer you will continue to face, for years to come, the need for much on-the-job training of potential managers and professionals.

PART FOUR

Promotion

INTERVIEWS

Nathaniel King

"You are dealing with people from a different cultural background with a different outlook on life," Nate King reminds his "brothers," discussing problems black people face that do not confront most whites in the white-collar ranks.

The education and training generalist at Allied Products Corporation in Chicago says he tells himself to solve such problems in this way: "Be myself. Have them accept me for what I am, and have myself accept them for what they are." He believes that present managers can better identify potential managers or professionals who happen to be black "by closer personal contact with them and closer observation of their performance." He advises white managers to achieve "closer personal and social contacts with potential managers or professionals to give them a better idea of what to expect and what is expected of them."

Unlike many Negroes, Nate King says, "Sometimes I think that present managers should treat Negro white-collar employees differently from any white-collar employees. The backgrounds of black white-collar people differ. Therefore, they should be approached differently."

Among his suggestions for different treatment is this: "Make the black white-collar worker feel at home and a part of the operation rather than an intruder. White-collar jobs for blacks are relatively new, and some blacks tend to think that they don't belong. Top management should erase all traces of that thought." King complains that present managers "discuss very little about the job with me. I simply ask questions constantly."

King sees these characteristics as essential to the Negro manager or professional: persistence, optimism, and willingness to learn and to accept setbacks. He adds that white managers and professionals need the same qualities, but not to the same degree as black people.

King points out that, in the long run, present white managers can help blacks progress in the white-collar ranks only to the extent that they are fair and avoid prejudice. From there on, it's mostly up to the individual. "He must work hard on his own to develop himself," he says. "Only the individual himself knows his problems best."

He urges more training for white-collar aspirants so that "they will get the necessary confidence to perform these jobs"; black people often lack self-confidence in this area because they lack a tradition in it. He draws attention, also, to the importance of acquiring some clerical experience and skill, even if the Negro aims much higher than a secretarial job. There's a certain clerical element in most white-collar positions, and it's well "to know your way around a typewriter and a file drawer, and to know elementary clerical procedures. You never know when they'll come in handy. And they give you valuable self-assurance."

Nate King was born in Mississippi on September 14, 1939. His father is a steelmill laborer and his mother a seamstress. He received a B.S. in chemistry from DePaul University. He and his wife have one child, born in 1966. His career has included stints as a food chemist and lab technician with the Continental Coffee Company in Chicago and as an assistant plant manager for the Richman Chemical Company in Chicago. He was also a foreman trainee with Republic Steel Corporation in South Chicago. Eventually, he plans to enter production management.

Wallace H. Kountze

"Significant changes for the better have taken place that now enable blacks to have rewarding careers in business and industry. Although hiring is still spotty, progress will continue to be made." So says Wallace Kountze, who since 1963 has been with the New England Telephone and Telegraph Company in Boston and is presently in the Public Relations Department as supervisor of urban affairs.

Although he recommends that a Negro go into the field for which his natural abilities best suit him, Kountze suggests sales for those with general, broad aptitudes because "salaries are good and job skills transferable." He points out that research and other technological fields are also promising. As to particular businesses, he recommends the communications industry—his own field—in particular, because "it needs black talent. This industry is now opening its doors to minority-group members and cannot hire enough blacks who possess the potential to achieve within the industry."

From his own experience and that of friends, Kountze believes that the Midwest and Northeast are the most hospitable sections of the United States for Negroes. But a discouraging factor is that all blacks everywhere "continuously have to prove themselves. There, too, is the 'invisible ceiling' everywhere, a limit as to how far a Negro can progress."

Wallace Kountze attempts to go above the "invisible ceiling" by trying to excel in his work assignments and to change assumptions of Negro inferiority. In this latter area, he has helped form a black caucus that seeks to plan and execute positive programs of action to "rid our particular business of racist practices." He has become convinced that black people in responsible positions must "agitate the establishment from within, continuously, by requesting that blacks be given employment opportunities equal to their capabilities at all levels within the organization." He suggests that white-collar Negroes can do this "by sharing experiences with one another and by encouraging those blacks in positions of authority to take leadership roles in their own firms and press for upward mobility."

At New England Telephone, Wallace Kountze feels handicapped, for example, because no Negro heads any department, at least at present. "I have no fellow black above me with whom I can relate," he says. "I want to discuss issues with someone who might have the power to change attitudes or practices within the organization." Thus he has to try to effect such changes, for the moment, through white managers, some of whom are "arrogant or have superior attitudes at best." He urges white managers and professionals "to take the time to learn and understand the real history of the black man and to treat him as they themselves would want to be treated."

Kountze offers these suggestions to the white manager who wants to bring more Negroes into white-collar jobs and help them win promotions:

1. Actively and earnestly recruit on predominantly black southern college campuses.
2. Work with blacks who are at the premanagement level to develop their managerial skills.
3. Assist blacks in learning all there is to know about their jobs.

In his own work as an urban-affairs supervisor, Kountze implements the company's commitment to improve the environment in which it operates. As part of such activities, he develops programs which serve to provide the minority community with meaningful types of employment, and he assists the School Department in its efforts to upgrade the quality of urban education. Better education, he believes, is the key to Negroes' advancement in managerial and professional ranks. He would recommend to his own daughters (born in 1955 and 1957) that they prepare themselves at a college of liberal arts, at the least. For men, particularly, he would advise graduate work, preferably in business administration.

Kountze himself will receive a master's degree in urban affairs from Boston University in 1970. He also holds a master's degree in education from the State Teachers College of Boston. His B.A.—in business administration—was awarded him by Western New England College in Springfield in 1963. He has also taken summer college-level courses in corporation finance, advanced psychology, and public speaking.

Kountze was born in 1931 in Boston; he served in the U.S. Army from 1950 to 1952, emerging as a corporal. He held jobs as a machinist in Massachusetts before starting college in 1958. While attending college, he held a full-time job and also worked part time as an administrative assistant at Western New England. He has financed all of his higher education with the exception of the master's program at Boston University, where his company is underwriting 75 percent of his tuition. Although he was 32 years old when he finally received his first degree, he found that it helped open job doors for him. He found his position with New England Telephone immediately after graduation.

Wallace Kountze believes that if he were white he would be at least one level higher than he now is and earning at least $4,000 more per year.

The Kountze family lives in a predominately black area of Medford, Massachusetts. It is satisfactory, he says, and he has no desire to live in a white suburban community, where, he believes, it is too easy to become a part of what he has been fighting. But he does not discourage other blacks from moving out—that is a matter of their own choice.

William R. Miller

Bill Miller has combined his engineering and teaching skills to build a place for himself in industry. Currently, as manager of corporate safety programs for the Goodyear Tire & Rubber Company, in Akron, Ohio, he uses both competencies to direct safety for the entire corporation throughout the country. And his double background also helps in some of his activities outside Goodyear—for example, he is a member of the Advisory Committee of the Vice-President's Task Force on Youth Motivation. Since 1965, he has been active in this area on a national level, visiting high schools and colleges to talk with students about the need for preparing to participate effectively in our economic society.

Miller is a native of Albany, Kentucky. After graduation from high school, he served three and a half years in the U.S. Army, emerging in December 1945 as personnel sergeant major of an engineer regiment. Then he worked for two years for a life insurance company in Muncie, Indiana. By that time, the G.I. Bill and funds provided by his parents had enabled him to enroll at Tennessee (A & I) State University in Nashville; in 1951, he received his B.S. in biology. He later received a master's degree in education from the University of Akron. He taught school in Albany in 1952–1953 before joining the Goodyear Atomic Corporation in Portsmouth, Ohio, in July 1953. He worked as a staff engineer in the Technical Division there until 1962, when he was transferred to the parent company in Akron. Here he assumed the duties of an instructor on the Training Center School staff until March 1965. He became assistant manager of the school then and manager less than a year later. Another promotion, to senior development engineer in systems research, lured him away from the strictly training side of the business. He advanced in that area to systems administrator, but in March 1969 he took the corporate safety position where he could combine his engineering and educational interests.

It is not surprising that Miller lists "competence, aggressiveness, and preparedness" as the most important characteristics that have furthered his career. He comments that such characteristics are vital for anyone in a white-collar job, regardless of race, but he believes that Negroes must "be more aggressive, persistent, and efficient" than whites to progress in such work. He advises: "Show initiative, be prepared, show achievement and hard work, and be demanding" of yourself and your superiors to win the advancement which you believe you merit. He believes that "everyone who has anything on the ball will almost be certain to get a chance, but you do have to make it on your own." He cautions, however, that Negroes need "the proper orientation to the real world of business."

Accordingly, Miller does not believe that Negro white-collar people should be treated any differently from other white-collar people. Nor does he believe that he has had any particular problems in dealing with either whites or blacks on a business level.

Bill Miller offers white management this prescription for identifying and promoting blacks as potential managers and professionals: "Maintain an open and objective mind (very difficult). Also, companies should have meaningful counseling programs."

He carries these ideas over into his extensive activities outside Goodyear. For example, he serves on the board of directors of the American Society of Training and Development and the American Cancer Society, and he is a member of his local draft board. He and his wife, Virginia, extend the philosophy to their family of three daughters, too.

Jonathan P. Nelson

"I generally imagine that all of the people around me are black and that their actions towards me are prompted by active senses of humor. I therefore react humorously, in most instances," says Jonathan P. Nelson, area plant engineer at the Brooklyn plant of Charles Pfizer and Company. He uses the technique when white coworkers are sometimes overbearing and when subordinates show antagonism by their attitudes and actions.

He has other perceptive comments about relationships between the races in business and industry: "Most black professionals seem to be qualified and possess all necessary credentials. But it is apparent that most employers want these black people to be 'acceptable' in white society. To enhance his chances for continued success, the black professional must develop interests that parallel those of his white counterpart. Any remark that implies 'black pride' is usually interpreted as a bent toward militancy and can be detrimental to professional advancement.

"Present managers can better identify potential managers or professionals who are black by evaluating the achievements and personality of the candidate and not worrying about the reaction of 'majority group' workers on said candidate's present level. I have known several potential managers who have been passed over because of the repercussions that might occur as a result of a minority candidate's advancement.

"An alarmingly large number of black people still do not believe that industry is truly sincere when it claims not to discriminate with respect to hiring and advancement. I feel that businesses need to hire a large number of minority-group members on all levels—particularly in the higher decision-making positions. This would serve to stimulate and motivate the white-collar black to be an outstanding achiever, because his top management 'soul brother' will be a living witness to the fact that black people can advance in the organization.

"The present white manager should not treat black white-collar employees differently from any other white-collar employees in evaluating job performance. However, I feel that present managers might try not to coerce the black to adhere entirely to the social mold of his white counterpart (bridge at lunchtime, drinks at the pub after work, attending the very white-oriented Christmas party, and so forth).

"The white professional is usually judged solely on the basis of his accomplishments and potential. I do not believe that evaluation of the white is nearly as subjective or severe as that of his black competitor.

"It is helpful to gain some knowledge of the particular company employing you. Very often knowledge of the company's history can give a candid picture of how its management thinks.

"I believe that any leadership potential that I possess has been largely developed by the various service and social groups that I participated in as a young adult (Boy Scouts, Omega Psi Phi fraternity, Canterbury Association for Episcopal College Students, and the Albuquerque, New Mexico, branch of NAACP).

"The characteristics I possess that have been most important in my career include determination and perseverance, a positive attitude, the ability to get along with most people, and a genuine belief in Christianity.

"The few blacks in white-collar jobs that I have known seem to perform acceptably. But I do advocate striving for excellence in all possible areas of the specific job. I also suggest outside study with the aim of moving a step higher than the present level. I strongly believe that supervisors and other superiors should be aware of the fact that an individual desires to move up.

"White managers can help blacks achieve promotions by being fair and impartial, making the black candidate feel that his efforts are genuinely appreciated, and not hesitating to promote potential black candidates when the opportunity presents itself.

"There really should be no necessity for a black person to prepare for office work differently from a white person. Knowing how to perform the job for which he or she is hired usually requires a certain amount of formal training in which a portion of the time is spent in the area of employability skills. Utilizing these principles and common sense are usually sufficient for coping with most office situations."

Jonathan Nelson was born in Harlem. His father was a railroad clerk with the New York City Department of Transportation and is now retired. His mother, also retired, was a seamstress and cook. The son attended New York City public schools and was graduated from Howard University in 1963 with a bachelor-of-science degree in electrical engineering. He has acquired credits at the University of New Mexico toward a master's degree in electrical engineering, but he now plans to switch his sights to a master's in business administration and will start graduate school in New York.

From 1963 to 1967 Nelson worked as an electronics engineer with ACF Industries in Albuquerque; from 1967 to 1968 he did similar work with EG&G, Inc., in the same city. He joined Pfizer in April 1968, having been referred to that company by Charles L. Fields Associates, a placement service. At Pfizer, in the company's pharmaceutical packaging area, he supervises packaging and maintenance mechanics and is responsible for evaluation, selection, installation, and operation of new equipment. His ultimate goal is to become an engineering manager, preferably in a technical service environment.

Nelson married the former Dorothy Elaine Higgins of Houston in 1968.

Jacqueline Pinckney

A Negro woman in business has two handicaps, her race and her sex, says Jacqueline Pinckney, manager of publications in the urban and public affairs operation of General Electric's Aerospace Group in Valley Forge, Pennsylvania. " Black women in business have to prove constantly to others that they are intelligent, competent, and not afraid of hard work," she says. "And they also have to cope with anti-feminists." She sees only one way to solve such problems: "Do your job as effectively and efficiently as possible, since results are what count."

Mrs. Pinckney readily acknowledges that sex and race are no longer drawbacks to getting an entry-level position. "But far too many qualified Negroes are stuck at the bottom rung of the corporate ladder. And they won't get unstuck," she adds, "until upper management pries them loose."

Jackie Pinckney graduated *cum laude* from the Philadelphia High School for Girls in January 1951, a month before her seventeenth birthday. Although she had taken a college preparatory course, she couldn't afford to go to college immediately. She took a clerical-secretarial job with the Provident Mutual Life Insurance Company in Philadelphia and attended evening courses at Temple University. She stayed with Provident Mutual for five years before joining General Electric in 1956. Despite the fact that she started with GE as a secretary, she moved into a professional job and eventually into a managerial position. Here's how she tells it.

"I entered the field of employee communications in January 1963 as assistant editor of the General Electric Missile and Space Division's weekly *Valley Forge GE News*. With no previous training or experience in journalism, I had to rely on inner resources, on-the-job training, and 'quickie' courses and seminars. I was promoted to editor of the newspaper the following year and given full responsibility for its content, production, and acceptance both by management and by employees.

"I was named co-editor of the division's quarterly magazine, *Challenge,* in August 1966, with attendant planning, interviewing, reporting, writing, editing, layout, and production responsibilities. My duties also included training and orienting incoming newspaper editors. I later assumed the full editorship of *Challenge,* and the job was expanded to include contributions to other ongoing employee communication-program activities.

"After being named manager of employee publications in March 1968, I supervised three editors and two clerical people in the production of *Challenge,* the employee newspaper, and a variety of brochures, booklets, newsletters, and so forth."

She believes that the same characteristics for success are essential for whites and blacks as managers or professionals in business or industry. She considers that the characteristics important to her own career are self-confidence, intelligence, aggressiveness, ability to get along with others, verbal dexterity, creativity, and an overwhelming desire to make her own way in this world. She says it is essential to "tackle any task; be constantly on the lookout for new approaches to getting a job done." She has used this formula as secretary, newspaper editor, and manager. "It has worked so well in the past that I see no reason to discontinue it now."

Mrs. Pinckney recommends her formula to potential Negro members of the white-collar ranks. But in addition she advises: "Learn as much as possible about the field, work hard, and swallow a lot of guff."

Once she saw the opportunity to enter the field of journalism, she enrolled in evening and Saturday-morning college courses in English, business, psychology, journalism, and other subjects at the University of Pennsylvania and Temple University. She has also studied at the Crowell Collier Institute in New York and has attended the American Management Association seminar for women managers. At the AMA course in 1969, she delivered the major address.

To the white manager of blacks she says, "Judge a person by assessing his skills, not his skin tone. If your employee is qualified to hold a higher-level job, give him the chance to succeed or fail. Let him know how he is to be measured, offer your help if needed, and then leave him the hell alone." She points out that the factors which motivate whites to succeed in business also motivate Negroes—money, prestige, and job satisfaction, primarily.

Mrs. Pinckney says she has no unsolvable problems in dealing with white associates and subordinates. "I treat them with courtesy and respect and expect the same treatment in return."

She likes her work and hopes to continue in public affairs, publications, and related activities. Because she is divorced, she has the prime responsibility of bringing up her son, David, born in 1958. She herself was born in Philadelphia; her father is a carpenter and painter, and her mother is a housewife.

Roosevelt Powell

"Beginning jobs for black people are available in the white-collar ranks, but promotion is the problem," says Roosevelt Powell, an engineer with the Northern Illinois Gas Company in Chicago. "White managers are moved up through the ranks until it is proved they cannot do the job," he says. "Black people are not." The Negro manager or professional has to "appear to be white or else be completely faultless."

Powell believes that white managers can help Negroes achieve promotion "by giving them responsibility to help them develop to their potential." He offers these other suggestions to present managers to help solve the problem of promotion: "Give the proper reward for a good job." Treat Negro white-collar employees differently from others in these ranks. "Black people come from a different environment and cannot be expected to perform the same as a white person in a white society." This different treatment should include, he believes, extended training to insure indoctrination even in such basics as the "language" of the office, which is completely unfamiliar to many blacks. Finally, management should offer special courses concerning the company's business, management training courses, and tuition aid to blacks taking business-related courses in colleges and universities.

For black people, Powell advises:

- Work hard and develop an acceptable personality.
- Acquire the necessary training to do a good job.
- Get experience, somehow, somewhere, in the office environment.
- Develop self-confidence and have the courage to make a decision.
- Be as natural as possible.

The last bit of advice stems from Roosevelt Powell's own experience. He finds that "naturalness" helps in his dealings with white colleagues. He advises: "Don't go around with a chip on your shoulder; be pleasant and willing to learn. But don't give up your convictions or be phony in order to please, because this will cause difficulties later on." He recalls talking about the riots over coffee one day with his boss. The discussion grew so heated that it affected their work relationship for a while. "But he had the problem, not me," Powell says. "Things eventually calmed down, and we ended up with a newer understanding of each other."

Powell was born on June 12, 1941, in Chicago. His father is a machinist. He holds a B.S. in mechanical engineering from the Illinois Institute of Technology. He got his present position through a black talent-search organization, Richard Clark Associates. He is married and is the father of four children.

Roscoe B. Robinson, Jr.

When Roscoe Robinson saw a help-wanted ad for a calibration technician at the General Electric electronic-tube plant at Palo Alto,

California, he applied—but without much hope. He had already been job hunting unsuccessfully for two months and had had no luck with a hundred written applications to California companies. Although he had not expected that his transition to civilian life from the navy would be simple, he had not anticipated as much difficulty as he was experiencing. Yet Roscoe Robinson got the job, largely because of his good navy record. While with the navy, he had served for six valuable years as an electronics technician on three ships and at the Naval Air Development Center in Johnsville, Pennsylvania (where he had also attended night classes at Temple University).

Less than five months after joining General Electric, Robinson won a three-grade promotion into the technician classification. Meanwhile, he had been offered jobs by two other companies, but he stayed with GE because he felt that the work offered him the best challenge and opportunity. That work remained substantially unchanged when General Electric sold the Palo Alto plant to Varian Associates, so Robinson became a technician for Varian. He has moved ahead with his new employer and is now a development technician, working with engineers in the development of digital systems used as part of a computer system.

He wants to progress to a supervisory position. "But I don't see a path to this end as a technician," he says. "I am also a licensed minister, and this calling may lead in other directions." He sums up his dilemma by discussing two problems peculiar to Negroes in business and industry.

"The first problem is simply that of being black. It becomes a burden to me and to people I deal with. It's sort of like wearing a large leg cast for about six months or perhaps having some deformity that is highly visible. In the case of the cast, you soon tire of the standard comments and questions about it, and you wish people could ignore it and just see you. You get tired of explaining it and making excuses for it, but you find that even you can't quite ignore it. If people don't make some allusion to it (this applies to the deformity, too), you can see by little give-away expressions or a slightly condescending manner that once again they see 'it' and not you. Then you realize—in the case of the deformity—that you are sort of conditioned and a little on the defensive about it, and you wonder how much of all this you are 'reading into' situations.

"This may sound supersensitive and absurd, but this type of

thinking is built into a person through many bitter experiences. Your mind develops a filter, and all your little day-to-day experiences are examined through this filter: 'Was he nice (rude) to me because of who I am?' 'Was I slighted because of . . . ?' 'Did he say that because of . . . ?' 'Am I really that good, or is he saying that because . . . ?' and so forth and so on.

"I have managed to come to terms with my filter, to a great extent, by anesthetizing it with a conscious effort and developing an oft-repeated philosophy—'So what if that is his motivation? I can only be me. If I bother him, that's his trouble.'

"The other problem, which is somewhat related to the first, may be unique to me—that of being just an *average* worker who happens to be black. As a technician in the electronics field, I find myself, as a black man, in a very small minority. Since there are so few Negroes in this field, the ones who make it are expected to be topnotch—'superpeople.' I am a contradiction because I am simply average. I am a good technician—good review marks, good raises on time—but I don't breathe and eat electronics.

"All through my 12 years in electronics, when people first meet me they expect to see some phenomenal knowledge or lightning trouble-shooting techniques, but they see only me—better than a good many I've worked with but not enough to dwarf anyone. When they find that I don't meet their stereotype for *the* Negro who has made it into an exclusive field, they figure I have just faked my way in and have made it on luck. They try to treat me accordingly. I sense this (or I think I do) and react in my own subtle ways and stick to my basic philosophy. Some never do become reconciled to their picture of me because they cannot accept me as just a technician."

Roscoe Robinson was born in Houston on June 26, 1938, just in time (he says) to interfere with his father's plans to become a doctor. The senior Robinson became a painter instead and now serves as a foreman at an air-force base. Young Mr. Robinson grew up in Richmond, California, the oldest of eight children. After an "undistinguished" high school career, he served six years in the navy, which he feels was "the making of me."

He and his wife, a registered nurse, have three children—a daughter and two sons.

Henry T. Sampson

"You don't solve problems of racial prejudice; you overcome them." So says Henry T. Sampson, a member of the technical staff, Power and Life Support Department, Applied Mechanics Division, at the Aerospace Corporation in El Segundo, California. Some of his prescriptions for overcoming racial prejudice are aimed at white managers and professionals:

- "Concentrate on overcoming your own racial hang-ups."
- "Evaluate performance of black employees objectively."
- "Avoid condescending attitudes toward black coworkers."

Once racial prejudices are overcome—or at least minimized—Henry Sampson believes progress can be made toward bringing more Negroes into white-collar jobs. He says that "a more aggressive recruiting policy, on-the-job training, and the guts to promote a qualified black" are particularly needed. Concerning the last point, he wonders how many white managers would have such courage.

Blacks can help by encouraging white management's energetic recruitment and promotion policies and by counseling blacks at college and high school levels on employment opportunities available in industry. But not many blacks, he believes, can help their fellows win promotions: "Not enough of them are yet in management positions to pull much weight." However, he disapproves of the inference that promotions should be made on the basis of race.

Despite his belief that racial prejudice is "ingrained in many white managers and professionals," he is optimistic about the white-collar future for members of his race. "Opportunities are available now and will increase significantly in the future," he says. He will definitely advise his young children to try for a managerial or professional career in business or industry when they grow up. (The Sampsons have two youngsters, born in 1961 and 1968.) In preparation for such a career, he will advise them to "acquire the best possible education now."

Henry Sampson's emphasis on education stems from his own background. His late father was dean of Jackson State College in Jackson, Mississippi, where Sampson was born in 1934. His mother is a retired social worker. Henry Sampson himself holds a B.S. from Purdue University and an M.S. and a Ph.D. from the University of Illinois.

His adult career began with the U.S. Naval Weapons Center in June 1956. He stayed there until August 1962, when he entered the University of Illinois. He came to the Aerospace Corporation in 1967, after an interview with a company representative. In his job, he is responsible for the highly technical synthesis and analysis of nuclear power systems for use in space. Aerospace is primarily a government contractor, having many contracts with the air force.

Henry Sampson is now sold on the West Coast as a place to live and as an area particularly hospitable to blacks. At this point in his career, he believes his salary and professional advancement would be about the same, regardless of color.

DISCUSSION

"Beginning jobs for black people are available in the white-collar ranks, but promotion is the problem." That comment by Roosevelt Powell succinctly states the challenge. Wallace Kountze puts it in these words: "There, too, is the 'invisible ceiling' everywhere, a limit as to how far a Negro can progress."

Blacks believe that, paradoxically, they hit the "invisible ceiling" on the job at the very time when they are making real social and political gains and showing significant economic progress. Judging by the standard of wages and salaries, more and more blacks are joining the nation's middle class. During the past ten years, the rate at which Negroes have moved into professional, technical, managerial, sales, and other white-collar positions has been quite dramatic. The Census Bureau has found that, in 1968, 641,000 nonwhites, 90 percent of whom were black, were working in professional or technical fields, compared with 9.7 million whites. That figure represents a 95 percent gain over the figure for 1960, compared with a 36 percent gain among whites. And it is expected that black families will keep shrinking the income gap between themselves and whites; already, the proportion of nonwhite families with annual incomes ranging from $7,000 to $15,000 has risen to 33 percent.

As the new black middle class grows, both in size and in self-awareness, an anomaly is appearing. Once, Negroes in the elite middle and upper classes of their race held a social philosophy much like this: "I made it by working hard. You can, too." But today that sounds like the white Protestant ethic; few middle-class blacks believe it, let alone voice it. As a result, the middle-class black has in many cases adopted far tougher, more assertive views, which come closer to those of less affluent blacks. A few decades ago a black middle-aged, prosperous manager, who had been with a large company for a quarter of a century, would have endorsed—perhaps even believed in—the systems of the white man. But now such a man advises his fellow blacks: "Be as aggressive as hell!"

How Blacks Can Spur Promotions

Asked about how to win promotions, the managers and professionals interviewed give advice that goes beyond mere aggression, of course. Ozzie Williams, for example, believes that, to qualify for managerial or professional jobs, blacks must:

1. Volunteer for tough, competitive assignments.
2. Constantly seek increasing responsibility.
3. Be prepared to work hard, recognizing the fact that for most whites success is the result of ability and hard work.
4. Develop empathy for fellow workers without reducing your own competitive drive.

But it should also be noted that Williams obtained his present job as manager of spacecraft development partly as a result of pressure by black employees on the management of Grumman Aerospace Corporation. Williams was a cofounder of the Big Brother Organization in Grumman, a group devoted to self-help by and for black employees.

Jim White puts it this way: "Black people must learn how to be aggressive, stoke up their ambition, and develop the techniques of in-fighting—how to come up with new ideas, how to guard their positions, how to associate with people who can help them. They must know how to walk a fine and sensitive line between aggression and tact, between persuasion and manipulation."

In Harvey Brewster's view, "black people can help Negroes win promotions by explaining how to avoid various job-related obstacles which face them as white-collar workers." Roscoe Robinson believes that the career path you choose can itself be an obstacle; he is not sure, for instance, whether the technical route he chose is the best way to become a supervisor.

Alex Murray points out that the black man should actively seek promotion, not expect it to fall in his lap. Charles Toney sounds another caution: "Don't let a psychology of defeat develop that affects both hiring and promotability." Do not be content "to indulge in self-adulation of . . . personal achievement," he also tells fellow blacks.

James Walton echoes the opinion of many managers and professionals interviewed when he points out that having more blacks in high-level management positions will prove "especially helpful" in priming the "promotability pump" for Negroes. He adds: "Expose them to better-paying, more meaningful, and more responsible positions."

How Whites Can Promote Blacks' Promotions

Many of the blacks interviewed believe that a major obstacle to their promotion is created by fears held by whites. Katheryn Lawson says that the best way white managers can help Negroes to achieve promotions is "simply by not being afraid to recommend them." Jonathan Nelson feels the same way; he points out that some white managers rationalize their failure to promote qualified blacks by saying that they fear "repercussions." Henry Sampson says to white managers, "Have the guts to promote a qualified black." He sounds the same theme as Walton, also, in his belief that not enough blacks yet hold management positions to pull much weight as far as promotions are concerned. On the other hand, he resents the implication that promotions might be made on the basis of race.

Williams advises white managers to help blacks achieve promotions "by steering them into key assignments and encouraging maximum effort and by preparing other whites to accept earned promotions on the part of blacks." John Walker believes that "present managers must remove their blinders. . . . A chance must be taken. They must move more blacks into responsible positions. Then they'll see motivation like they've never seen before."

A second obstacle to promotion, those interviewed believe, is lack of objectivity. "Just be fair," Mark Grant urges white managers. Durant Brockett asks for "advancement criteria weighted only on the basis of the individual human being." Charles Butler feels that present managers can better identify potential managers and professionals among black people through an honest appraisal system and by utilizing sound management development. "Promote strictly on ability without regard to race," he pleads.

Alex Flamer says that white managers can help by "explaining what is needed to get ahead, by being honest, and by demonstrating a positive attitude in showing that they really want to see Negro advancement." Chuck James points out that white managers can help Negroes achieve white-collar promotions "by judging blacks by the same criteria they use to judge whites and by encouraging blacks who they think possess management potential." And he adds: "Treat blacks no differently from whites."

Wallace Kountze thinks something must be done to encourage objectivity; accordingly, he has helped to form a black caucus that seeks to plan and execute positive programs of action that will "agitate the establishment from within, continuously, by requesting that blacks be given employment opportunities equal to their capabilities at all levels within the organization."

The men and women interviewed noted a third obstacle to promotion: the shortage of specific programs aimed at helping to promote the black man within the organization's white-collar ranks. Kountze and Williams approach the problem by means of organized activism, but most white-collar blacks appear to favor either individual activism or more passive and conventional methods. Mark Grant is an example of an individual activist: He believes in exploiting every new position he has held for its educational value, and he has done this so successfully that he is now in Rio de Janeiro as a data-processing consultant for International Telephone and Telegraph's South America Computer Division. Others, like Art White, Durant Brockett, and Jerry Tudos, use their individual activism to go into business for themselves. Tudos formed Career Systems, a professional and technical placement firm, because he felt that opportunity wasn't knocking loudly enough for him in organizations owned and managed by whites.

Phil Jones, however, believes that there is outside help to improve the promotion situation for blacks. After experience with a placement firm, he advises white managers: "Enlist the aid of professional, psychologically oriented specialists to help overcome prejudices." He adds: "Be fair. Accept leadership ability and skill regardless of color." Jones sometimes concludes, from his more somber experiences in the placement field, that "a Negro may look black, but he has to act and think like a white man to win advancement with some employers."

Nate King prescribes a specific program to spur the promotion of blacks: "Closer personal contact and closer observation of their performance." Dick Lawson also indicates that present white managers must know blacks better. And Bill Miller says, "Companies should have meaningful counseling programs" on what it takes to win promotions.

Gerard Peterson advises white managers to "use tailor-made programs to motivate black people in white-collar jobs." He advocates "a new frame of reference in identifying potential managers or professionals. Discard stereotypes—don't look for a Madison Avenue type or an Ivy League background. Have an open mind, but not an empty one, when examining the important requirements for management."

How Am I Doing?

In essence, the prescriptions of King, Miller, and Peterson seek to provide an answer to the question "Where do I stand?" All employees—white and black—want the answer, but blacks probably look for it more urgently than whites because they have less tradition in white-collar jobs. Although they say they want—and indeed do want—more promotions, they are realistic enough to know that promotions can't come every day, or even every year. What they really want is some kind of periodic appraisal or other signal that tells them where they stand.

Few blacks will ever put the question to you, a manager, as baldly as "How am I doing?" Actually, some may never ask it even indirectly. They are restrained by their natural inhibitions or by experiences as minority-group members, which have taught them never to expose themselves to the possibility of a direct rebuff. But you should provide an answer whether or not the question is asked. You can channel, you can teach, and you can motivate blacks if you reply correctly. Withhold the answer, and you will end up with aimless, discontented, and probably disgruntled white-collar blacks.

How can you best answer the question? No formula exists, but the elements in your situation, and your own skills, will determine the right method. A few possibilities are the formal appraisal, the motivational technique, and simple intuition and empathy.

The formal appraisal. The formal appraisal won't be the best way to answer "How am I doing?" in all cases, but it can often be helpful. Ideally, the appraisal session takes place annually. The boss talks over with the employee his performance since the last session. They should have a position guide to use as a measure against the actual performance. Supposedly, out of this come readable signals that a Negro white-collar worker can follow to improve himself on the job.

Unfortunately, this procedure gets more talk than practice in American business, because, when tried it sometimes has been found wanting. Here's why: Effective appraisals require real training and competence. Even a graduate psychologist sometimes finds himself hard-pressed to conduct a worthwhile interview; since few managers have degrees in psychology, it's scarcely surprising that they experience trouble.

Another difficulty with formal appraisals has to do with the reaction of the person who is being appraised. He "hears" the positive side, but the negative gets across to him less clearly. As a result, the appraiser can achieve only some of his objectives. Then there is the fact that often the manager himself remains skeptical about the worth of appraisals. He conducts them because he has to, but his attitude is conveyed to the employee, and the whole performance degenerates into a charade that neither party can take seriously.

Yet another drawback is the position guide. The person being appraised may not perform as the guide stipulates, because it was written when someone else had the position or because the job has changed. And finally, most appraisals apply more to the manager than to the individual supposedly being appraised. The corollary of this is that many people perform as they are managed—good management means good performance, and bad management, bad performance.

Is the formal appraisal, then, worth the trouble as an answer to our burning question? Yes—it has worthwhile uses. If the manager is properly trained in the use of the appraisal, it can become a valuable tool. Good appraisals should transmit information, influence attitudes, and influence skills. A manager who is a competent interviewer can make broad evaluations with the appraisal—for example, he can decide an employee is very good, fair, or poor. And, depending on his own skills, he can make even finer evaluations. Also, the good appraisal interview can serve informational purposes for the employee. It can report to him in general terms how he's doing, especially in positive areas. The degree to which negative areas are brought out depends on the skill of the appraiser.

In a large organization, where a manager may supervise so many people that he can't give much personal attention to many of them, the appraisal serves a valuable purpose. It can make up for the lack of the day-to-day personal touch.

But probably the greatest benefit of a good interview is that it can stimulate the employee to appraise himself. If the manager is skillful, he will get the employee to think and talk objectively about himself, so that he actually appraises himself—especially negatively. When the interview turns to self-appraisal, the manager should show sympathy and encouragement. The best approach is to be an "active" listener. Let your man pour himself out, but channel his expression so that he actually discovers himself.

Advice for appraisers:

1. *Be ready for each interview.* Review the employee's record ahead of time. If you don't know him well, get opinions on him from others. If you must make some difficult comments, rehearse them.
2. *Put the black white-collar worker as much at ease as possible.* He will probably be nervous. At first, talk about impersonal

subjects—business conditions may serve. Slide over to the personal side by saying something positive about his performance.

3. *Discuss your purpose.* Even if you have both participated in appraisals before, remind him that this is a regular procedure, not some special griping session or a complimentary discussion preparatory to your announcement of a promotion or raise. If the timing of the appraisal and a promotion happen to coincide, so much the better. But keep money out of this discussion. Reserve compensation for another, special talk.

4. *Give the black man or woman a chance to speak.* Ask questions and wait for the answers.

5. *Make standards and goals clear.* You should try to do this by encouraging the employee to formulate them. If they need correction or change, discuss why.

6. *Ask the employee to say how he thinks he measures up to the standards.* Praise those strong points on which you both can agree, and discuss the weak points as objectively as possible. Let these develop from what the employee says. Even if he doesn't directly admit his faults, you can usually work into them from something he has said. Here's an example: "That remark you made a minute ago about time is perceptive. We all have trouble managing time—with deadlines, for instance. You did well on the Jones job, but I noticed you got a little behind on the Smith and Johnson assignments. . . ."

7. *Develop ways to improve.* Emphasize the employee's capacity for improvement. If possible, draw attention to previous periods when he has shown improvement. Also, stimulate his own ideas for improvement. Make it *his* program, not something imposed from above.

8. *Tell the employee he can come back any time to talk—and mean what you say.* Too often, the "open door" policy proves a "closed door" practice. If the door remains shut after an appraisal, you have lost more than half the value of the interview.

Watch your manner during the appraisal, particularly the following aspects of it:

1. *Relax. Take your time.* Arrange to have no interruptions,

especially by telephone. If this is difficult, conduct the appraisal after hours.

2. *Give the impression that your opinions can change,* especially on the negative aspects of the appraisal.
3. *Stimulate discussion.* Avoid a wrangle if the employee shows signs of becoming argumentative. Change your judgment with good grace if he can present some facts about a negative point which were previously unknown to you.
4. *Keep your guard up.*

Watch out for the man who agrees with you too readily, who won't talk much, or who won't open up. With the too-agreeable employee, give voice to some opinion with which you know, or are reasonably sure, he does not agree. With the nontalker, try simple silence —it can work wonders. With the person who won't open up (this is by far the most common problem with blacks), probe for his opinions, and keep at it until he does begin talking. Often, the pump merely needs a little priming.

When you end the appraisal:

1. Review the salient points.
2. Reassure the employee of your continuing interest.
3. Determine, with the employee, what remedial course should be followed.
4. Discuss any job-related matters he brings up.
5. Stop when you both have said everything. Don't prolong the discussion unduly.

The appraisal interview sometimes leads to unexpected results. Hitherto unknown facts may turn up. In one session, a young accountant with a disturbing degree of absenteeism revealed that his invalid wife caused the problem. The interviewer later discreetly verified this, and the two worked out a way to make up the lost time. In another session, a manager gave such a glowing appraisal that the employee asked for a raise on the spot. The supervisor had to explain hastily that he reserved money for another session—he should have explained that at the beginning. At the opposite extreme, particularly negative appraisals have led to more than one resignation on the spot. The manager should be prepared for this possibility.

If the appraisal session does reveal dramatic new facts, an adjournment is often the best course until you can absorb the new information—and also verify it. A raise is certainly implied when you give a good appraisal, and you gain credibility if you give one at a later session. When you must give a bad appraisal, don't let the person appraised work himself into a corner where the only exit remaining is resignation. If you think he is salvageable, say so—and explain how. If not, try to suggest some job possibilities which might suit him better. Find something positive to say.

A final word of warning: Control the natural impulse to counsel on off-the-job matters; if they bear on job performance, deal only with that aspect. For example, the manager we mentioned above properly advised the employee with the invalid wife how he could make up his lost time, but he did not touch on how the employee should handle the invalid. The appraisal should relate strictly to the job of the person appraised. Few people are qualified or trained to discuss family problems, psychological quirks, or personal difficulties. Even if you are asked questions, avoid such subjects.

The motivational technique. If properly used, the motivational technique stimulates people to do well. When a person knows he's performing capably, the question of how he's doing becomes less urgent to him because he knows and is comfortable about the answer.

Douglas McGregor, in his book *The Human Side of Enterprise,* makes six assumptions he considers valid in motivating men:

1. Man spends his physical and mental effort naturally and will apply it as readily at work as at play.
2. Control and the threat of punishment aren't the only ways of getting people to do things.
3. Commitment to objectives is as strong as the attraction of the rewards associated with their achievement.
4. Under proper conditions, the average person accepts and seeks responsibility. When he doesn't, such behavior usually results from bad experience, not inherent human characteristics.
5. Creativity is widely, not narrowly, distributed among human beings.
6. Man's capabilities are only partly used.

Western European and American society is moving toward ends based on these six assumptions. Examples are in the freer attitude toward children, the changes in husband-wife relationships, and the improved status of minority-group members.

Assumptions 3 through 6 are of the greatest significance for blacks as they strive to break into the white-collar ranks of industry. What factors will stimulate commitment, encourage the acceptance of responsibility, unlock creativity, and make fuller use of capabilities possible?

The following facts bear study:

1. *Man is a wanting animal.* His wants are never really satisfied. If they are satisfied at one level—hunger, for instance—new wants must take the place of the satisfied ones. Satisfied needs do not motivate; unsatisfied needs do motivate.
2. *When physiological needs are satisfied—hunger, shelter, and so on—the next level of needs takes over as motivators.* These are "safety" needs—the desire for fairness, freedom from tyranny or favoritism, and assurance of fair administration.
3. *Next come the social needs*—friendship, love, acceptance by peers.
4. *The fourth level consists of the ego requirements*—recognition, status, and self-esteem.
5. *The highest level is the need for self-fulfillment.*

The business community succeeds fairly well in satisfying needs on Levels 1 and 2, but it does progressively poorly from then on up to Level 5, which is seldom satisfied. On Level 3, white managers are particularly remiss in dealing with blacks; most white managers commonly adopt an "arm's length" relationship that rarely suffices to meet social needs. Managers resist dealing with blacks on Level 4, too —indeed, this resistance is extended to whites as well. The word "ego" has an unfavorable connotation. But managers would be wise to recognize that blacks hunger for self-esteem and recognition as much as whites do. If you can give it to them honestly and legitimately, why not do so?

Managers face their greatest challenge in encouraging the self-fulfillment of their employees, white and black. This is a private, individual matter. A manager, of necessity, must limit his role to providing the proper conditions for self-fulfillment—an atmosphere in which his employees know they can advance on merit, know they have the freedom to fail, know that better jobs await them if they do well on their present one.

In the motivational approach, you discuss goals with your people. You establish a rapport about purposes and ways and means to achieve them. The "How am I doing?" question is answered almost automatically during the course of such talks.

When a manager uses the motivational approach well, he comes to know the limits as well as the potentials of his people. Many a supervisor has overrated an employee—white or even black—and then wondered why a promotion didn't work out. Because there is now pressure in business and industry to integrate blacks into the white-collar ranks, the temptation to overrate grows stronger. You can resist it best when you know your black employees.

You answer the "burning question" best for blacks (and everyone else) by discovering what motivates them best. The intensity of the burning question, for most employees, is in direct proportion to their dissatisfaction with their own performance or their own job slot. Remove that dissatisfaction by motivating more effectively, and you will cool the question off a little.

The intuitive, empathic technique. The method of intuition and empathy is closely related to the motivational approach for letting an employee know how he is doing. "Empathy" is putting yourself in someone else's shoes, feeling his emotions, suppressing your own emotions and ego in the effort to share temporarily in his. This is always difficult, and it is especially hard in the typical white-black relationship, but it can be done. For example, it was probably empathy between the white manager and the black accountant that led to the revelation about the invalid wife.

Intuition and empathy don't just happen. They are capacities that must be developed, and two of the best ways to develop them are to be honest and to listen.

Honesty does not mean being brutally frank. It means revealing part of yourself to another by showing some of your own emotions and attitudes. This won't prove simple. Besides the barriers of race, you must overcome lifelong habits which have probably taught you to hide your true feelings. We often hide our feelings because we have learned that a close friend may sometimes be as much a burden as a bitter enemy. But, if we want empathic understanding, we must accept the burdens of friendship.

Affirming the Negative

What should a manager do when he must pass over a black employee for promotion? What should he do when he must censure—a far more common case? Do the same thing he would do with any employee: Face up to the issue. First, make sure that the censure or lack of promotion is deserved. Next, talk it over with the employee. Never ignore the situation, hoping it will blow over. It's more likely to blow into something more serious if the employee is not told exactly where he stands. Here are suggestions on how to do the job right:

1. *Keep criticism—direct or implied—impersonal, private, and fair.* Talk about the job, not the person. If you know your man is prone to take things personally, emphasize other respects in which he has performed well.
2. *Listen.* Evaluate the employee's explanation for his sins of omission or commission and accept as much as possible.
3. *Do not delay your censure.* Do it as soon as possible after the situation arises. But don't be hasty. Give advance thought to your course of action.
4. *Do not delegate to others the task of explaining or reprimanding.* The person reproved will interpret such delegation as cowardice on your part, or as evidence that the error is not serious or that you have a bad conscience about the situation.
5. *Do not be apologetic about the situation.* The employee will react just as if you had delegated the disagreeable task.
6. *Be positive in your reprimand.* Say why the error is serious or why the employee is being passed over for promotion.
7. *Avoid ultimatums,* except in extreme cases. They put both you and the employee in a corner. The ultimatum usually proves unnecessary.
8. *Assure your employee of your continuing respect for him* if you can honestly do so. Underscore the fact that you differentiate between shortcomings and the individual as a whole.
9. *Follow up.* See that the error doesn't recur, and be sure that a passed-over employee still functions well despite his disappointment. In the latter case, compliment him on his continued good performance when you can honestly do so.

The manager who gets the best from his employees—white and

black—is the one who can best create an atmosphere of approval within which his group can function. To do this: Develop performance standards and set them high enough to stretch your employees. Measure performance against the standards. Let people know where they stand—above, at, or below par—and develop remedial action with employees who perform below par.

In an atmosphere where an employee knows exactly where he stands, he is happy and free to unleash his full creativity. Neither soft good fellowship nor the authoritarian approach is involved. But justice is very much involved. That's really what the black (or white) employee asks for when he asks about his status.

PART FIVE

Stabilizing Employment

INTERVIEWS

John H. Chadwell

John Chadwell is a college professor turned businessman. He had no intention of leaving the educational field, but the director of personnel relations at Owens-Illinois, Inc. invited him to join the company as assistant to the director of human relations in May 1968. He has held the position of director of human relations since August 1969, and he now has no intention of leaving the business world. He hopes eventually to win promotion to the executive level of line management.

"Business and industry are now ready for us in managerial and professional jobs," he says. "It's up to us to meet the challenge."

Not that he believes problems don't still exist for Negroes in white-collar jobs. He cites three that particularly annoy him:

1. *The pressure for quick success.* He finds that both whites and blacks expect instant evidence that he has "made it." In his work which contains so many intangible factors, it's particularly hard to show tangible results. Chadwell is responsible for developing and coordinating programs throughout the company to attract, assimilate, train, and retain members of minority groups. He is also responsible for educating and counseling all levels of management in this area and presenting and improving the corporate image. Success in such areas does not come quickly.

2. *The limited margin for error.* The nature of Chadwell's work is such that some errors are inevitable. Some minority-

145

group people quit; others don't assimilate; managers sometimes misunderstand policies. But Chadwell feels these failures even if they are unavoidable. "Maybe I'm oversensitive," he acknowledges. "A white man in my job, with my temperament, might feel the same as I. But somehow I think there would be a little wider margin for the white man."

3. *The usual bias with which blacks are confronted in varying degrees.* However, he acknowledges that his white colleagues are "generally helpful, with measured friendliness."

Chadwell solves such problems "through the reduction of dissonance as the situation indicates or demands." He says: "The key to dissonance reduction is the establishment of a posture of freedom. Since I was aware that there may have been some resentment to my presence, I used every opportunity to dispel the myths associated with hatred and bigotry by attempting always to be well prepared, friendly, and free. Confrontations with bigotry provide opportunity as well as frustration. I cannot guarantee that any attitudes which were negative have changed, but behavior has been almost totally exemplary."

He urges Negroes now in white-collar jobs to encourage others to apply and to recommend them to supervisors. Chadwell advises present white managers and professionals "to eliminate double standards on salary, promotion, and responsibility."

He believes that Negroes should take advantage of the present social climate to get as good a foothold as possible in industry. He believes that the present demand for minority-group members in "human relations" jobs will subside eventually, although some demands will always remain.

His expectation is that, once the Negro finds a spot in the white-collar ranks—no matter where—he can eventually find a place for himself closer to the mainstream of business. He advises his brothers to "keep pushing; pressure helps."

Chadwell will definitely advise his one son (born in 1954) to pursue a business career if he wants to, because "equal opportunity is the law of the land. It must be implemented—both because it is the law and because of the more liberal social climate." His major piece of advice to his son: "Get a good liberal education and then develop a specialty."

John Chadwell was born in 1923 in Toledo, Ohio. His father is dead, and his mother is retired. He went to secondary public schools in Toledo; then received his B.A. from Alabama State University in liberal arts and his M.A. from Columbia University in education. For thirteen years he taught at Claflin College in Orangeburg, South Carolina; Albany State College in Albany, Georgia; and Alabama State in Montgomery. He has also had three years of government service at local, state, and federal levels.

Henry Helm

"If you're black, you can do better financially in some jobs, such as personnel work or marketing, than if you're white," says Henry Helm, pointing out a paradox in today's white-collar job market.

For example, he believes that in his personnel position with General Mills, Inc., in Minneapolis, his income would be lower by at least 13 percent if he were white. "I know it doesn't make sense," he says, "but discrimination never has made sense. Here's a rare case where we are benefiting—temporarily, I believe—because of today's climate, in which social and legal factors are at last forcing integration. I might add that, although this country still has a long way to go to achieve integration, business is making an effort and is ahead of some other 'establishments' in America."

His advice to white managers and professionals: "Forget about our being black. Look upon us as just trying to do a job." His advice to fellow blacks: "Show Whitey that we can produce."

Helm gives this advice to blacks because he finds that the major obstacle to wide acceptance of Negroes in managerial and professional jobs lies in the lingering belief of whites that blacks can't do the work. Therefore, he urges his fellows: "Do any job 100 percent. We blacks face a sales challenge. We're kidding ourselves if we think every rebuff is just racial discrimination. Some of it may be prejudice concerning our abilities. Every black who personally proves that prejudice to be false helps the cause. Every black who performs poorly on the job hurts the cause and harms our collective chances to break through more completely into white-collar areas."

Henry Helm speaks from experience. Before joining General Mills, he spent four years as a teacher and counselor. Now he interviews and selects people for engineering and technical positions. He won his own job as the result of an employment agency's contacting him. He likes personnel work and hopes to remain in it. Currently, he's working on an M.S. in psychology from the University of Minnesota. He was graduated from Lincoln University in June 1964 with a B.A. in sociology and psychology.

Helm was born in 1942 in Jackson, Mississippi. His father is a waiter, and his mother is dead. He and his wife are the parents of two children, born in 1960 and 1969. He will advise his children to try for white-collar jobs in business or industry when they grow up because "this is where the money is." He would urge them to prepare themselves by attending college, majoring in engineering, and also obtaining a master's in business administration.

He believes engineering and science offer the best future for Negro youngsters in this technological era. He would suggest manufacturing industries, particularly in the northwestern part of the United States, as the most hospitable for blacks—the Northwest because its social climate is the most favorable for Negroes and manufacturing industries because the government and social pressures in these industries help to win fair treatment for blacks.

His parting word: "White managers can help bring more Negroes into white-collar jobs by inviting more in for interviews and by evaluating them as individuals, not as blacks."

William M. Outlaw

"I am not sure that this problem (getting more blacks into white-collar jobs) can be solved without a complete restructuring of society," says William M. Outlaw, a computer programmer with IBM. "The problem of white racism has not been solved," he explains. "What I have attempted to do is seek out those employers who seemed willing to allow me access to the higher-level positions in their companies." He thinks that some companies are beginning to relax their discriminatory policies, but that these companies are few.

Outlaw emphasizes that the great majority of companies still discriminate in their hiring and promoting policies, and that it is these companies that pose the fundamental problem. The next most serious problem is the "misuse of the black man's talent once he is hired. The employer must adopt the policy of promoting managerial talent even though the possessor of that talent is black. If present management used the same criteria for identifying black potential managers as for white potential managers, the number of black managers would increase. It's as simple as that," he believes. And he adds with some bitterness, "The white man can be confident that any talent he may have will be recognized; the black man can be confident that in most instances his talents will not be recognized."

Further, Outlaw makes the point that most whites can count on much managerial and professional training after they are hired. Although some blacks may now receive the same treatment, most still have "to acquire their training prior to being hired." Therefore, he says, "Potential black members of the white-collar ranks must have as their goal the acquisition of some type of formal training. Without it, the black man leaves himself more open to continued rejection." This fact of business life accounts for the seemingly "checkered" careers of many blacks who now hold white-collar jobs. Often, they were refused promotions because of color, so they had to move on.

Along with the "job hopping" image, the Negro who becomes a manager or professional also typically has or acquires the characteristic of aggressiveness. "The successful black manager," Outlaw notes, "has an almost inhuman determination to overcome all obstacles no matter how insurmountable they appear." He adds: "The white manager can best help the black employee by removing the racial obstacles to promotion. I think that performance and motivation are proportional to opportunity. The black employee will be motivated when he sees that he can advance if he has the necessary qualities. He will perform if he sees that he will be rewarded for his performance. Once the white employer opens all lanes of advancement to the black man, there will be no question of motivation."

Before joining IBM's one-year computer programming and training course, Outlaw had three years of experience in private accounting and four years in tax accounting. During those seven years, he went to college full time; he received a bachelor's degree in business administration from Pace College in New York City, where he was in the top quarter of the class of 1967. After his IBM course, he became a programmer with the corporation in Poughkeepsie, New York. He plans to move eventually from the technical area of programming into management, and he also intends to obtain a master's degree in management.

William Outlaw was born in September 1938 in North Carolina. He is married and has one child, born in 1966.

Gerard M. Peterson

Gerard Peterson was born in Hartford 36 years ago. His father is a welder, and his mother is in housework service. He spent his early years in the Hartford vicinity until he enrolled at the University of Connecticut. His education was interrupted by a two-year tour of duty in the U.S. Army; after his discharge, he returned to school and, in June 1957, received a bachelor's degree in economics. Having a firm belief that extracurricular activities are important in developing a student, he participated in several areas. As president of his college fraternity and chief announcer of the campus radio station, he began exercising his interest in community affairs.

Immediately after graduation, he joined the Aetna Life & Casualty as a computer programmer trainee. Through a series of promotions including jobs as senior programmer and senior systems analyst, he attained the position of administrator of selection, education, and training for the Computer Division. During this time, he received his CDP (Certificate of Data Processing) from the Data Processing Management Association as the result of a qualifying examination.

While serving as a member of Vice-President Humphrey's Task Force on Youth Motivation, he was loaned by his company to spend a year in Washington, D.C. As an administrative coordinator for the Plans for Progress program, Peterson traveled more than 90,000 miles to all major urban centers in the United States and organized programs to stimulate cooperation among the business community, university representatives, and public school administration officials. In addition to his other duties, he was the cochairman of two national conferences held in Washington to promote equal education and equal employment opportunities.

After his stay in Washington, he joined Aetna's Group Insurance Division as a marketing representative. In September 1968, the Board of Directors appointed him assistant secretary of the Group Division.

As a corporate officer of his company, Peterson still finds time to pursue community activities, including being a director of Big Brothers of Greater Hartford, the Community Renewal Team, and Connecticut Talent Assistance Cooperative. As a member of the Health Care Facilities Planning and Capital Region Mental Health Planning Committees, he is able to use his experience in health insurance to help develop future programs for the metropolitan area. He is also a member of the Governor's Council on Youth Opportunity and the State Council of Correction. As the chairman of High Noon's Education Committee, he maintains constant contact with many educators and students. In cooperation with NAACP, the Urban League, and other community-based organizations, the committee assists in solving the many problems of the urban schools.

Peterson suggests the following fields as most promising for black people who aspire to managerial or professional jobs: economics, data processing, accounting, and sales. The best way to get a job, he believes, is through black employment agencies, the Urban League, and direct contact with placement directors.

Characteristics he considers essential to the Negro manager or professional include intelligence, energy, articulateness, innovativeness, and driving ambition. He emphasizes the last quality and believes that a black person must be more ambitious than a white to make comparable progress. Peterson says that he has always had to be "willing to walk an extra mile" to get ahead.

He offers this advice to present managers who sincerely want to help blacks advance: "Use tailor-made programs to motivate black people in white-collar jobs. Develop summer and cooperative training programs or any other approach that helps black employees understand and become part of the *real* office environment."

He advocates "a new frame of reference" in identifying potential managers or professionals. "Discard stereotypes," he urges; "don't look for a Madison Avenue type or an Ivy League background. Have an open mind, but not an empty one, when examining the important requirements for management. For instance, the best candidates for the top management for a company like J. C. Penney may be more like the customers than past administrators have been."

He believes that good, fair-priced housing in substantial neighborhoods is the main problem for the manager or professional who is a minority-group member. Another problem is achieving a style of living comparable to that of his white associates, as in clubs and similar activities. To solve these problems, he advises, "Insist upon the use of every means possible to push the black man into every traditionally exclusive institution."

Although he has already moved forward in his career, he has even more ambitious plans. He wants to achieve a top-level management job and ownership of a substantial part of a business enterprise.

Peterson is married to the former Carole Minor of Newport, Rhode Island. They live in Bloomfield, Connecticut, with their two sons, Brian, aged 11, and Bradford, aged 4.

Louise Prothro

"I certainly do recommend that more blacks get with it, or we as a race will never enter the mainstream in industry. Unfortunately, I know that a lot of black parents have not equipped their kids for a competitive society. I am afraid that, with the new emphasis on special grants and special programs for blacks, we are building more defenses against the necessity of competing."

So says Louise Prothro, consumer market specialist with a New York public relations firm, Farley Manning Associates, Inc. "Bringing more black people into jobs is a dream of many black people already in the field," she says. "There has been some hesitancy until recently because blacks have felt insecure and preferred to remain 'the one and only.' We are only now realizing that there is strength in numbers." Mrs. Prothro points out that it is still difficult to persuade Negroes in teaching, law, medicine, and other traditional occupations to enter business because "many in these areas have the feeling that such a profession is the epitome of success, as indeed is true in many communities."

She adds that she "would advise anyone to go into industry who has the aptitude and the dedication to do so. I think, however, that young people will be much less tolerant of whites' stereotyped attitudes toward blacks and less malleable. Yet maybe they level more readily, and maybe that is what's needed. I would advise first that every young person open up to new ideas and customs. I recall that as a child I was told to 'look and absorb.' I felt the family was treating me as though my head were a sponge, but it worked. And I have noticed in industry that a white newcomer adjusts much more quickly than a black. Perhaps, in this day of proving that 'black is beautiful,' we overlook the fact that we can become too conspicuous and fit out of rather than into the mainstream of activity."

In the final analysis, however, Mrs. Prothro believes that at this time "the whole problem of bringing more blacks into industry lies primarily with white managements at all levels. First, they have to have the desire and determination to bring blacks in. Then they have to recruit them in the right places—with success, not failure, in mind. They have to grade and upgrade Negroes on merit and nothing else. They have to make sure that the rest of the white personnel get the message and follow through with conviction."

Mrs. Prothro believes that the problem of women—white and black—in management and professional jobs equals the problem of blacks in industry. "I am sure I face the same problem all women face in managerial positions; men simply do not see women as effective in management. Frequently we are in the position of helping the latest boss understand what the department is all about. We are pigeon-holed as women and as specialists."

In her field of public relations and home economics in industry, there are many women but few Negro women. For many years, she was the only Negro in an all-white group. "It is a bore," she says. "The sole Negro in any situation is expected to be a synthesis of all Negroes. One is constantly called on to interpret actions of all Negroes—the janitor to the secretary to Whitney Young to Rap Brown. It is sort of like wearing a yoke, and it is difficult to perform to one's best advantage when the role of being *the* Negro is forced upon you."

Louise Prothro also explains that the black community does not understand the role of a black person in industry. "Therefore, one is expected to be somewhat of a showpiece to be considered successful in black circles. I don't want to be considered good 'as black.' I am good in my field, and I ask evaluation on that basis alone. In the same way, I do all that I can to fight problems as a professional worker and not as a black. I want both whites and blacks to consider me as a professional, not as a black. For reasons such as these, I shudder when I hear about all the bizarre methods of 'readying' one of my 'brothers' or 'sisters' for a job situation."

She says that a Negro should get ready for a managerial or professional job in the same way a white does. As a start, this means acquiring the necessary education and preliminary experience for it. Once in the desired field, she believes, "it's a matter of doing the job better each time and of constant attention to your own personal goals, desires, and familial allegiances." She adds: "And it is perhaps knowing whence one comes. I mean that in the broadest terms. Being black is no new thing with me. I grew up with stories of accomplishments of blacks from around the world. I have old books with tales of Pushkin, Dumas, Matzeliger. I was made to understand the statue of Attucks in Massachusetts, the significance of the man who ran to establish the capital of Oklahoma, the contributions of Drew at Howard and with the blood bank. I know the history of my family, who left Georgia when the black-white thing was too big for them. And I have had books that describe how blacks were written out of the history of the areas from which they came."

In the years she has been in public relations, promotion, and marketing, Mrs. Prothro says, she has usually been met with courtesy and genuine friendliness. "When there has been an air of incredulity that I am Negro or curiosity about how I made it 'as a Negro,' I have resented it. Such attitudes imply amazement that a Negro could be in this arena. I set the record straight when it is suggested that I have a unique background. It is not so."

Mrs. Prothro was born in Macon, Georgia, the first child of parents who are now dead. The family moved to Connecticut when she was only six months old and later to Worcester, Massachusetts. Her father was a successful salesman for a New England firm. His Negro heritage was not generally known until his daughter graduated from college—Framingham State, near Worcester, where she received a B.S. in home economics in 1941. Her first job was as an assistant dietitian in a women's prison. Louise Prothro also holds an M.A. from Columbia University in foods and nutrition and has taken various other courses in Boston, North Carolina, and St. Louis. In 1943 she married a young medical student at Howard University, Joseph Robinson, Jr. Their one child, Joanne Robinson, was born in 1946. A graduate of Bennington College in Vermont, Joanne now teaches and works in modern dance in Boston. Dr. Robinson died in 1948. His young widow married Charles E. Prothro in 1951, just as she was finishing her work at Columbia. The Prothros moved to Atlanta, his home. There Mrs. Prothro joined the Pet Milk Company, which was her introduction to industry. She was with Pet, in Atlanta and later in the home office in St. Louis, from 1951 to 1968, when she joined Farley Manning, which had been handling the Pet public relations account.

At the agency, she works with all the accounts in the Women's Interest Division—planning public relations program research, recipe development, and photography; writing releases and feature story materials; handling editorial contact with national media; making radio and television appearances; and giving lectures and demonstrations, in addition to acting as special market counsel for all accounts in the agency.

Charles W. Toney

Charles Toney has spent 23 years in the Deere & Company organization, the first farm-equipment company to exceed a billion dollars in sales. Currently, he carries the title of manager, minority relations, and provides guidance and counsel to company representatives on all matters where the interests of minority groups are concerned. He represents Deere at Plans for Progress and EEO meetings and seminars, is responsible for EEOC compliance reports, and serves as contact man with state and federal agencies on matters concerning training, housing, and educational programs for minorities. He joined the company as an arc welder at the John Deere Plow Works in Moline, Illinois. Over the years, he has held various positions with the corporation: as personnel representative, training representative, and personnel development representative. He is now in Deere's corporate headquarters in Moline, Illinois.

Toney recommends to young black men and women entering college that they concentrate on technical professions if they have the aptitude for them because the job opportunities in engineering, science, and accounting are growing the most rapidly. Blacks are now living in an age of unlimited opportunities in disciplines other than the traditional "sacred, safe four"—teaching, preaching, law, and medicine. He suggests farm and industrial equipment, auto manufacturing, steel, and office equipment as promising industries for job opportunities.

Toney considers his native Midwest (he was born in La Crosse, Wisconsin) as a good area for a Negro as far as employment is concerned. He believes all parts of the nation except the South are about equally hospitable to the Negro manager or professional. He strongly urges that blacks aim more at the private than at the public sector, because the private sector, more than any other part of our society, is applying the cutting edge of change to our pressing social problems.

The greatest handicap to a Negro today in winning white-collar status, he feels, is the fact that "ghetto living contributes little exposure to business practices and opportunities." Therefore, Toney urges blacks to "acquire the education to compete." (He regrets that he himself does not have a college degree, and he feels the college education he did acquire was beneficial when promotion opportunities did occur.)

Charles Toney makes the point that a black person can "psyche" himself out of a promising business career by "failing to be proud of his black heritage and allowing a psychology of defeat to develop that affects both his hiring and promotability." For those reasons, he advises young Negro adults "to be as aggressive as hell!" Discrimination and some form of racism will never be completely eliminated in America, he believes, but a black man can handicap himself by using race as an excuse every time he misses a promotion or a chance at a job. Enough companies are committed to equal opportunity that one rejection should not be considered a defeat, and even white professionals interview many companies before offers are made and a decision is reached.

Toney also points out that black people themselves can help bring more Negroes into white-collar jobs if those who already are managers and professionals show the advantages of such careers "by their own examples of accomplishment and achievement." The black professional performs a disservice to his fellow black Americans if he adopts the "I've got it made" philosophy. He adds, "I will never be personally satisfied until every black boy and girl in Mississippi has the opportunity to acquire the education that will equip him to be employed and perform to the limit of his own personal capabilities. In my opinion, it is the responsibility of black managers and professionals to address themselves to this problem and not indulge in self-adulation of their own personal achievement."

To white managers and professionals, Toney offers this advice for better relationships with Negro colleagues: "Learn more about black history and culture. Try to evaluate blacks as individuals and rely less on myths and stereotyped conceptions."

It's really simple, he says, for white managers to help bring more Negroes into white-collar jobs: "Hire them." But he acknowledges that because of past and present second-class citizenship, special training and development may be necessary at first to help blacks win promotions.

Charles Toney has no complaints about his own housing situation, and he hopes for another promotion or two before his career with Deere ends. Advancements have come along with fair regularity during his near-quarter-century with the company. Although he has received "no overwhelming invitations to join private clubs," he believes his business career currently is not harmed by his color. "Presently, for a comparable position," he says, "my color has nothing to do with any wage differential. It is the extent of my capabilities that counts."

"I am egotistical enough," Toney says, "to feel that if the employment opportunities had been as open for my generation as for the present one, I would now perhaps be a vice-president or president of a company."

Charles Toney advised his son to enter business "because this is where the action is, and I see color as no obstacle to advancement or financial remuneration." The son is an industrial relations representative with John Deere East Moline Works and was recently promoted to be the assistant to the industrial relations manager.

Jerome G. Tudos

"Make your own way," Jerome Tudos advises fellow blacks who want to progress in the business world. He has followed the counsel by starting his own business, Career Systems, Inc., in Washington, D.C.

As president, he runs an organization specializing in professional employment consulting. CSI provides services in minority-group recruitment and placement and in college recruiting. It assists in professional and technical placement through the use of its computerized manpower register. Résumés are preprocessed and screened according to job specifications indicated by its client firms.

Jerome Tudos started his firm in January 1969, because he felt that opportunity was not knocking for him in organizations owned and managed by whites. In working for white-dominated operations, he often found the attitudes of his white colleagues toward him "condescending and gratuitous."

Career Systems, a small but growing enterprise, now employs six people. Tudos financed it from personal and private resources and does not think that the government's Small Business Administration "is really prepared to deal with black entrepreneurs . . . at this time."

Tudos believes that blacks who aspire to white-collar work should pick the industry or profession that suits their individual exposure, motivation, or drive. They should *not* choose a business or profession only because it appears at the moment to offer more hospitality to blacks.

Black people can help other Negroes join the white-collar ranks by "holding fast together," he believes. And white managers can further the cause by judging blacks' qualifications "on the basis of performance and merit." Tudos' advice to white managers and professionals for better relationships with black colleagues—"get out of the way"—is less harsh than it might at first appear. By this he means: "White managers and professionals must discontinue their gratuitous and condescending attitude toward black professionals and step back and allow us to perform our professional services and functions, as we are qualified to render them, to the best of our individual talents and abilities."

Jerome Tudos was born in 1942 in Salem, New Jersey. His father is a factory foreman, and his mother is a nurse. He received his B.S. in physics and mathematics in 1965 from Morris Brown College in Atlanta, Georgia; his education was financed by scholarship and personal resources. He has continued graduate work at Catholic University in Washington.

After graduation from Morris Brown, he worked as a civilian physicist for the Navy at the Naval Ship Research and Development

Center's Aerodynamics Laboratory. He left there in 1968 to join Computer Sciences Corporation as a systems analyst.

Tudos does not believe that he would ever consider working for another employer. His explanation: "The obvious advantage of self-employment is that one can excel at his own rate of development, building and creating his 'own thing.'"

Bernard Walker

"Give blacks a chance to prove they are qualified. Take them out of the 'special' category. Stop making excuses for blacks in white collar ranks that sound like EOC guidelines. Stop using oddball federal compliance provisions. Give blacks opportunity because they fill your needs. Let them compete on an equal basis. Let them make decisions and take their lumps." That's the advice Bernard Walker gives to white managers and professionals for better dealings with their black colleagues. To fellow Negroes, he makes these suggestions to help their brothers get more white-collar positions and win promotions: "Tell the truth. Make them believe they owe themselves the real facts. Urge them to pursue what they want, not what they expect."

Walker fears that the current climate of opinion, powerfully augmented by the government's equal employment laws and procedures, will distort black people's views about the job situation in business and industry, especially for white-collar positions. This climate, he fears, may distort the actual job (and already has done so in some cases), making certain types of work "Negro positions."

Bernard Walker was promoted from sales promotion manager to personnel manager of the Carnation Company's Houston Fresh Milk and Ice Cream Division in 1969. A graduate of Southern University, Walker majored in graphic arts and received his B.S. in 1949. He was a supervisor in adult education with the Veterans Administration and did graduate work at Texas Southern University before entering the service for a two-year stint with an army education training unit. In 1953, he joined Carnation as a sales management trainee in Houston; he became a territorial salesman the following year, and in 1967 he became sales promotion manager.

In his personnel job, he and four assistants are concerned with the areas of management training, personnel administration, labor relations, safety, health and welfare, and work simplification coordination. About 80 percent of his personal time is spent in labor-management relations. Eventually, he hopes to work at the corporate level in labor relations and contract negotiations.

To a young black man or woman coming out of college, Walker would recommend blue-chip industries and companies because "they're sophisticated and up to date. Young blacks should have the chance to look at modern concepts today and not get stuck in some obsolescent situation with the need, eventually, to catch up."

Bernard Walker is only half joking when he says he would advise his five sons and daughters to get into some sort of trade or vocation rather than a professional position. "Trades and vocations are short of blacks," he points out. "I hope my sons want to be master plumbers or electricians. At present there seem to be greater fraternity and money in the trades. The inequities, moneywise, between labor and management favor the trade vocations, at least for now."

Because so relatively few Negroes do his kind of work, he feels a little lonely now in his white-collar job, even though he gets "invited to everybody's house party." He explains: "Because of my position and color, I have to be 'best,' not 'better.' I get identified as 'black' first, despite my position, status, and calling card. A black tradesman is more readily accepted by whites than a black manager. Whites are friendly enough to me, often overfriendly—but they're critical, too, often overcritical."

Walker solves such problems "by knowing more about my 'white friends' than they know about me. I let them polish the apples. My advantage is that experience has taught me when I'm going to be punched full of holes."

Born in 1928 in Houston and a long-time resident there, Walker acknowledges that "blacks perhaps have more to overcome, or prove, in the South." But he adds, with an optimism characteristic of him,

"Once you actually break the Mississippi Curtain, you can make it anyplace."

Unlike many Negroes, he does not believe he would be earning more if he were white. "I earn more than the white person I replaced," he explains. "Housing is not my hang-up, either," he adds. "A man ought to live where he's comfortable, and I do. I live with my family outside the Houston city limits in an area that could be considered undeveloped and disadvantaged for my status. Nevertheless, I'm sure I want to live there. I don't believe many black managers have a true problem here—because most don't really know they're for real."

Walker has one final bit of advice to blacks who want to get ahead in the white-collar world: "Acquire an education, of course. Get a haircut often and don't wear dirty tennis shoes."

Arthur M. White

Art White owns a distributorship for Anheuser-Busch brewery products in the Lawndale-Austin area of Chicago. He opened for business on August 18, 1969, having obtained the distributorship partly because he is black. "The disorders in Chicago helped me," he acknowledges. "If I were white, I would not have acquired an Anheuser-Busch distributorship—or at least not one in a ghetto area."

However, Art White had several other things going for him, besides being black. He had been with the St. Louis-based brewery for 15 years in marketing capacities before he became a distributor. "While with the parent company," he recalls, "I had years of experience dealing with the black community. My customers knew that all my promises and dealings would be final because I was backed to the hilt in St. Louis." Because he comes from the ghetto himself, he points out, he can "communicate to ghetto residents in their own language."

And, in addition, he gets along well with white business colleagues, whom he describes as "generally helpful and friendly."

White employs 11 people in his business, which has a capitalization of $250,000. Discussing his business plans for the future, he says that he hopes "to expand his area as far as possible." In running his own operation, he has encountered many of the problems any small businessman meets—employee turnover, finding qualified employees, competition, and the like. But one problem—financing—plagues him to a greater extent than it does most white businessmen, he believes.

For this reason, he urges more young black men and women coming out of college to choose banking as a career: "This would be the salvation of blacks. We may be fortunate enough to have knowledge about a particular business, but we often lack the financing." He urges young people to try to choose their profession early, so that they can get a head start in their education for it.

Art White deplores the "sponsorship" route to a career that many blacks are now forced to follow. He explains that today a bright young Negro makes substantial career progress most readily when he's lucky enough to find a sponsor—an individual (sometimes white), corporation, or organization. The sponsor usually doesn't come forward until a person has already shown signs of ability, and this may not occur until he has reached maturity. Thus he has lost some valuable and irreplaceable years of his life. Furthermore, the sponsorship system is uncertain, quixotic, and somewhat demeaning. Art White points out that white artists, writers, musicians, and similarly gifted people had pretty much abandoned the patronage road by the end of the eighteenth century.

He also has some unusual advice to Negro youth on where to begin their business careers—"in Detroit, Chicago, Newark, or other cities where the major racial disorders occurred." His reasoning, borne out by his experience, is that riot-torn communities are more ready and eager, even, to accept black businessmen than other areas.

White believes that industry can be the salvation of the inner cities. "Industry left the inner cities, and that departure caused many of the present problems. Industry has to return to help black people, but it has to have blacks in its management."

To present white managers and professionals, he offers this advice: "Recruit blacks from colleges and start them with salaries equal to those of whites who have the same jobs. When better positions are available, promote on a fair but competitive basis. Offer the same training advantages to blacks and whites alike."

Art White urges blacks already in white-collar jobs to help bring more Negroes into their ranks "by continued pressure on companies that only want to 'showcase.' Lay out your program and don't be afraid of the repercussions." Yet blacks need more than militancy to integrate white-collar areas more completely, he believes. Present white-collar Negroes should "teach black neophytes company policies, make certain they are not neglected, and explain the incentives available for a job well done, for this is what motivates men."

White would advise any of his four sons or his daughter to enter business. But first he would recommend college, then "learning every phase of the fields that they go into."

White had 15 years at Anheuser-Busch to learn his field, but he also spent three years with the American Tobacco Company before that, when he served his apprenticeship in consumer selling. He once taught and coached basketball for a year in high school.

White was born in 1927 in Chicago, the son of a laborer and a housewife. He received a B.A. from Loyola University in Chicago.

DISCUSSION

William Outlaw points out a characteristic of some blacks who aspire to managerial or professional careers in industry: their checkered job history. He and others interviewed emphasize that Negroes often move on when they are refused promotions because of color.

In the past, opportunities have been so scarce for the black professional that, when he found a job, he usually stayed longer than his white counterpart. But increased opportunities, coupled with increased aggressiveness and awareness, have caused the younger professional to be less tolerant of inequities on the job. "The ambitious black has an almost inhuman determination to overcome all obstacles, no matter how insurmountable they appear," says William Outlaw. He advises that present managers discount checkered job histories and remain undaunted by the appearance of aggression. "Once the white employer opens all lanes of advancement to the black man," believes

Outlaw, "there will be no question of motivation. He will perform if he sees that he will be rewarded for his performance." Bob Jenkins adds that ending the double standard applied to whites and blacks in industry would result in more job stability among blacks.

And, of course, by no means all Negro managers and professionals have checkered job histories. Charles Toney has been with one employer, Deere & Company, for 23 years. He says a black man can handicap himself by using race as an excuse for every instance of a missed promotion or unfair treatment, real or fancied. There are enough companies now committed to equal opportunity that one rejection shouldn't be considered a defeat.

Art White was with Anheuser-Busch for 15 years before opening a Chicago distributorship for the brewer's products in 1969. Gerard Peterson, in his late thirties, is another example: He joined Aetna Life upon graduation from college and has been with that insurance firm ever since.

The Nature of Turnover

Yet turnover among white-collar Negroes is probably higher than among whites. For example, one nationwide company experienced a 31 percent annual rate of turnover among all white-collar employees, but the rate was 29 percent for whites and 42 percent for blacks. Even after allowances are made for a statistical anomaly (that percentages rise faster when the base number is lower), the higher rate for Negroes is disquieting.

Each potential manager or professional who quits costs the employer at least $1,000 in out-of-pocket cash. The total expense is much higher—it is estimated to be as high as $5,000—because the employer has lost a man who possibly could help run the company in later years.

Some turnover, however, is probably desirable. Research studies have revealed that low rates of turnover are associated with low rates of profit in stable, slow-growth businesses. This suggests that too much stability, as indicated by a low rate of turnover, may lead to lethargy and competitive flabbiness in a business organization.

A real possibility exists, then, that if an organization goes for an extended time with too little turnover it may lose its vitality and stagnate, either for lack of fresh blood or for lack of opportunity to practice adapting to change. A certain amount of turnover is also necessary to provide developmental openings for present employees in the form of opportunities for promotion and upgrading. Too much turnover may lead to decreased productivity, but too little may interfere with the essential task of developing new talent. Some sort of dynamic balance seems to be required.

When we refer to turnover, we usually mean payroll turnover (as we did above)—that is, separation from and addition to the payroll. However, an even more significant type of turnover, especially for white-collar jobs, is *position* turnover.

Studies indicate that job tenure of 18 months to 4 years is the zone of optimal productivity for most positions. However, this may vary widely, depending on the type of business involved. In any case, there is bound to be some position turnover. In fact, where one fairly big position is vacated, it is estimated that a chain reaction results involving as many as six changes.

Retirement will claim some employees. Many more will inevitably be attracted to other employers by higher wages, more interesting work, better working conditions, or the promise of greater advancement opportunity. This applies to both whites and blacks.

The need for additional manpower, particularly at the higher skill levels, which an expanding economy normally requires and an expanding technology virtually guarantees, must be met by readying people through a more or less graduated series of jobs. Normally, each job requires little more than improvement of the skills which were partly mastered to reach an acceptable level of performance, plus the acquisition of new skills along the way to achieve the quality of performance ultimately desired in this job or necessary for the next promotion. Thus interpositional movement of people within the organization is essential to motivate growth and to develop the talent needed to meet expanding needs as well as to replace talent lost through upgrading or turnover. High turnover, paradoxically, can be both a threat to stable productivity and an imperative for development.

How to Reduce Turnover

In discussing turnover among black white-collar workers, we must keep two things in mind: First, some turnover is inevitable and even desirable. Second, most Negro newcomers to the managerial and professional ranks will be quite recent college graduates—a factor which virtually guarantees turnover. About 15 percent of college graduates with nontechnical degrees change jobs by the end of their first year in the business world; after five years, only some 60 percent are with the same employer they joined at graduation. On the other hand, of all technically trained college graduates, 9 percent have left their first job by the end of the first year; after five years, 63 percent are still working for the company that originally hired them. These are the findings of Dr. Frank Endicott, director of placement at Northwestern University, whose studies included both whites and blacks. The data for blacks show more job hopping than those for whites.

The exit interview. The first requirement for reducing turnover is to know the facts. How much white-collar payroll turnover do you have? How much position turnover? Is your payroll turnover too high or too low? (An average of about 35 percent is considered normal in these days of a tight labor market.) Good payroll record keeping can develop the statistics, but it won't reveal the reasons why people leave. An exit-interviewing program can accomplish that.

A skillful interviewer and good questions determine the success of the exit interview. An effective exit interviewer should have the qualities of a good counselor. He generally should not be a manager or anyone else with an "authority image," because departing employees, especially blacks, will not open up to him as readily as to a more neutral person. Often, the employment interviewer can handle this job well. This has these added advantages: The interviewer gains insight into the characteristics of employees who are likely to terminate; and he also learns more about specific work situations, which can help him make better placements in the future.

To conduct the exit interview:

1. *Prepare properly.* Make an appointment. If possible, schedule the interview in advance to allow yourself time to prepare. Review the case in advance, plan your approach, and arrange for privacy. Assure the departing individual that his remarks are confidential.
2. *Establish the proper atmosphere.* Use a friendly, permissive approach. Start with small talk and move only gradually into the major subject. Maintain a nonthreatening climate. Assure

the employee that the situation he is participating in is not judgmental.

3. *Use a constructive approach.* Never ask for criticism. Most people will not criticize openly because their lifetime habits and training make them feel they must be positive and say only good things about people. Therefore, even if an interviewer does ask for criticism, he usually won't get much. Rather, he should request suggestions for improvement. The departing employee may readily identify areas of dissatisfaction if he can phrase them positively and constructively.

4. *Gain the confidence of the employee.* Demonstrate responsible, objective treatment of information. Many departing employees fear that negative comments may somehow reach the ears of the next employer, so they need reassurance. Tell the departing worker that his comments and suggestions will be treated as privileged information. Maintain an atmosphere of confidence. A sympathetic approach helps. And don't take notes during the interview. Instead, after the interview, summarize your impressions.

5. *Work from the general to the specific.* Start with a general question, such as a request for comments on working conditions in the organization. Often, this will quickly lead to specifics. If not, start asking leading, more direct questions about areas of particular interest, such as supervision or training.

6. *Remain completely permissive.* Agree; don't challenge or argue, even if the departing worker makes outrageous statements. Let him do the talking. Keep your comments as impersonal as possible. For example, don't ask for opinions about "your supervisor." Ask about "the supervision."

7. *End on a positive note.* Demonstrate your appreciation for the helpful information received. This is especially important, because the departing worker has probably revealed more information and opinions than he had intended.

8. *Document fully.* Put your impressions in writing while they are still fresh—but do this after the interview, not during it.

The interviewer should concentrate on obtaining three types of information: reasons for leaving; name of the new employer and the factors which made that company more attractive than the present one (only, of course, when the departing worker already has a new job); and attitudes—regardless of the worker's stated reasons for leaving—toward pay, opportunity for advancement, work content, and management actions or policies.

Getting such information is seldom simple. That's why a written questionnaire rarely brings satisfactory results. For example, the separating employee hardly ever has any strong interest in seeing that the working conditions of his old job are improved. If they are bad, it hardly matters; he is leaving them behind, probably because he has decided no hope for improvement exists. Therefore, he may be somewhat cynical about discussing them at this late date. Normally, all he wants is to make the break cleanly, without needlessly burning his bridges or antagonizing anyone who might turn in a negative reference on him later.

If a company finds it impossible to conduct personal interviews, the next best alternative is an anonymous questionnaire to be mailed in. Such a questionnaire usually reveals more often than an interview that people have quit because of dissatisfaction with management actions or policies: 5 to 10 percent is the normal proportion in exit interviews, compared with 15 to 25 percent in anonymous questionnaires. Exit interviews, however, tend to produce much more detailed and broadly useful data and to cover a larger proportion of separating employees.

Also, don't overlook another possible way to obtain information from a separating employee: an interview by telephone with him several months after he has left. Some of his objectivity may have returned by then; furthermore, he will have had time to compare the realities of his new job with his old job. However, time may have blunted some of his old impressions, or he may fail to be objective about his new job, especially if he has begun to realize he may have made a mistake in changing.

Information may also be obtained from the separating worker's former manager through a personal or telephone interview or a written response to some form of questionnaire. The former manager's estimate of the reason for leaving can serve as a useful cross-check against the interviewer's own impressions. The manager's objectivity may be suspect in some cases, particularly if minority-group members depart from his jurisdiction with suspicious regularity.

One final word on exit interviewing: Assure the interviewer himself that his findings will be used and will be treated objectively. More than one interviewer who has reported disagreeable opinions and facts emerging from his exit interviews has had the data buried or even used against him. And you can hardly blame an interviewer for suppressing or sugarcoating derogatory findings about management after an unpleasant experience or two.

The attitude survey. You don't always have to wait until an employee quits before finding clues about turnover. Periodically, you should check all employees regarding their satisfaction with pay, advancement opportunity, job content, and management actions and policy. To be noted particularly are any differences in responses between black and white employees.

In anonymous attitude-survey questionnaires, people generally will say whether they are considering a change of employment soon. Check to learn whether the percentage indicating such an intention approximates the actual turnover rate. Often, it does. Such surveys thus offer you the opportunity to practice preventive medicine in employee relations.

You can gather this kind of data in several ways. The easiest is the anonymous attitude survey, which can be administered to groups of employees on the job and collected immediately or handed or mailed out to be completed voluntarily at the employee's leisure and returned at his discretion. Note here especially your rates of return— black versus white. If the return rate for blacks is significantly lower than for whites, the probability is that your Negro employees fear reprisals. Even if that fear is unwarranted, you have a communication task ahead if you want to allay it.

You can also gather data on attitudes by means of personal interviews. The disadvantages of this method lie in its expense and the difficulty of getting candid responses. However, a skilled interview can offset the latter problem, and it is offset by the fact that you can acquire more and deeper data and opinions.

Manpower Planning: Critical Task for Management

Once you have your statistical facts from payroll data and less tangible information from interviews or questionnaires, you can start on the key factor in keeping blacks on the job—manpower planning.

Any company, large or small, is in the manpower-planning business whether it wants to be or not. It may perform the function well or poorly, depending on how skillfully and seriously it meets its obligations. Every firm today, if it wants to survive and if it wants to conform with the law, must include in its manpower planning a program for hiring blacks for managerial and professional jobs. If it wants to keep those it has recruited, it must plan how it expects to do so.

Job stability among your Negro white-collar workers won't just happen. You must take steps to make it happen. Manpower planning, performed well, offers these advantages:

1. It will give managers more flexibility in conducting their business.
2. It will help you obtain and keep better people.
3. It will give employees—black and white—a greater sense of accomplishment and stability.

A manager who practices good manpower planning provides for continuity in his operation by developing "second men" for key positions. By looking ahead, he can minimize the peaks and valleys in his operation, thus stabilizing employment.

Stability and continuity in the organization give the manager greater opportunity to conceive and take on new projects, improve productivity, and increase quality. Without good manpower planning, a manager may have to spend much of his time "fire fighting"— that is, trying to solve each manpower problem as it arises.

With good manpower planning, a manager should consistently have better people working for him currently than he did a year earlier. Thus he should be able to promote from within his own organization when vacancies occur; and, when he must make cutbacks in his operation, he can seek to place people elsewhere.

Above all, good manpower planning enables a manager to keep a high proportion of his people from voluntarily leaving.

When the manpower function is planned, employees themselves are more comfortable. They welcome the sense of purpose and the knowledge that stability is one of the objectives. Training is a factor contributing to the goal of giving employees a sense of accomplishment and stability. It multiplies the skills of employees and thus contributes to the first objective we mentioned—greater flexibility in the organization.

Four steps are essential in good manpower planning:

1. *Set the target.* Get a complete picture of the unit's market forecast to determine the direction the manpower program should take.
2. *Take stock.* Learn about past productivity rates, employment levels, and turnover rates as well as the present composition of the organization's managerial, technical, and other workforces by experience, age level, and potential. The black employee is part of the overall picture you are interested in, and that picture will strongly influence his own decision to stay or leave.
3. *Make a yearly projection.* Use the data obtained in Step 2 and project your figures one year ahead on the basis of marketing forecasts.
4. *Use the projection.* The best planning and charts in the world are useless if they are not put to work. Take action in recruiting, selection, development, retirement, and training to meet manpower problems revealed by the forecast.

A large company with an extensive drafting department surveyed its manpower requirements for ten years ahead. Among other things, it learned that 20 percent of the draftsmen would retire over the coming decade. In addition, another 15 percent would probably quit, to judge from past rates. At the time, the company had no black draftsmen, so it set out to recruit them on a planned basis. Furthermore, it told its black candidates about its plans. "The fact that we had a plan laid out for ten years ahead impressed the black draftsmen," said the department's manager, "and contributed importantly to our hiring the cream of the crop. When the word about our plan got out, we found many Negro draftsmen—and there still aren't too many of them—applying for our jobs. In short, the plan served as a recruiting device, a function we had not at first dreamed it would perform."

Perhaps the most important step of the four is number 2, taking stock. Under this comes recruiting and hiring (which have been discussed already in the chapter on that subject), appraisal (discussed in the chapter on promotion), and identification. While we have already touched on identification in our discussion of promotions, we can add some further comment here.

In identifying talent, you also need to project ahead to estimate how you will use it. A good device is the so-called "5 x 5" program. In this, you identify the top and bottom 5 percent of your black employees in white-collar positions, on the basis of performance. The top 5 percent should be tapped for eventual promotion; the bottom 5 percent for salvage operations. Such a program forces the manager to reward the better performers and to do something constructive about the poorer performers. Such a selective analysis can be a powerful tool for minimizing unwanted payroll turnover.

Some managements look upon manpower planning as window dressing that they can do without, yet all companies perform this function whether they realize it or not. Since you must do it, why not do it well? These four steps will help to insure success:

1. *Get top management support.* The top manager in the component must support the program fully, or it will never get off the charts and forms into action.
2. *Get managerial support at all levels.* When the general manager approves, the next step is to enlist the wholehearted backing of all the other managerial echelons.
3. *Communicate fully and frequently about manpower planning* —don't hide its light under a bushel. There is much communication about marketing and equipment goals. Manpower should be no exception.
4. *Go "first class."* Give the manpower-planning function status in the organization and staff the activity with good people. Give it visibility. Manpower planning can determine the future direction of the business. To do the job right requires the best in people, budgets, and support.

The three S's. Good manpower planning assumes that you give attention to satisfying the black employees' requirements for salary, supervision, and status.

Many—though not all—of the people interviewed believe they would be earning 10 to 20 percent more if they were white, given the same abilities. A few think they earn more because they are black. But they all believe that the employee should be paid on the basis of his ability, not his race. You should therefore review your personnel policies and pay practices to see how they may be bettered to insure equitable pay for blacks. You should measure these policies and practices against principles of salary administration that many authorities believe should include the following:

1. *A fairly determined evaluation for each position.* The first step is to describe correctly the duties and responsibilities for each position. The second is to assign a level to each position; this may be done on the basis of some type of ranking, classification, point system, or factor comparison.
2. *An orderly grouping of similarly evaluated positions into salary grades.* A salary grade is a grouping into a common salary range of jobs involving approximately the same difficulty. The jobs within the grade can vary, but they should all have about equal salary value.
3. *A minimum and maximum salary limit for each salary grade.* This is necessary because salaried positions are subject to more variation in performance than are most hourly jobs. A single rate with automatic increases allows insufficient recognition of individual differences in performance. A good pay structure provides ranges wide enough to reward employees who perform well.
4. *Sufficient difference between grades to recognize real advancement from one grade to another.* For instance, a difference of 10 to 15 percent between the minimums, midpoints, and maximums of two adjacent salary grades is sound. The percentage difference between any two adjacent levels should be about the same.
5. *Minimums and maximums that are competitive.* The only way to achieve this goal is through an area survey. Many local employers' groups conduct such surveys on a confidential basis.
6. *A salary structure in line with the wage structure.* This principle will prove especially significant in keeping black managers and professionals on your payroll. A common complaint is, "Top hourly people earn more than I do." Salary ranges must be adjusted as changes take place in hourly scales.

A final word on salary administration: Review each white-collar worker periodically—semiannually if possible, but at least once a year. Try to keep merit increases separate from raises stemming from general adjustments. Many firms set 7.5 percent of the base salary as a sound merit increase. Grant a raise of more than 10 percent only under exceptional circumstances.

Good supervision is the second "S" that will help keep blacks—and whites—on the job. The following ten good supervisory practices may seem self-evident (some of them have already been mentioned here); but, through carelessness or ignorance, they are frequently not adhered to.

1. Praise publicly; censure privately.
2. Give credit when and where it is due.
3. Let each employee know how he is doing.
4. Let people know about changes in advance.
5. Make the best use of the black employee's abilities.
6. Delegate responsibility.
7. Be considerate.
8. Lead, don't drive.
9. Listen to your black managers and professionals.
10. Get to know them better.

The third "S"—status—involves recognition of the black as an individual, giving him a feeling of belonging and imparting to him a sense of accomplishment and a feeling of security. All employees crave status regardless of race, but blacks in particular require it because so many of them have been without it for so long. There are a number of practices that will improve both status and job stability for your black white-collar workers.

First, there is *training*. We have said a great deal about this in the training chapter, but now we should add that blacks object particularly to a condescending approach. And the "canned" program often inadvertently gives an impression of condescension. Tailor your training to your own circumstances and to the needs of your black managers and professionals.

Personal development and advancement are obviously important. Our comments in the chapter on promotions need only this addition: Many of your black employees may want to continue their formal education through university extension courses or other means. They will welcome your cooperation and encouragement.

In addition, each black employee needs to understand the lines of *responsibility and authority* and the decisions he can make on his own. These are matters you must spell out clearly. Make readily available accurate and clear position descriptions and policy manuals. Employers tend to limit blacks' authority unnecessarily.

All employees, including blacks, have *complaints* from time to time. Keep your door open. Let everyone know you will listen to legitimate complaints and try to remedy them.

You should give blacks the same *personal freedom and privileges* that you give whites in similar positions. Avoid policies and practices which tend toward regimentation (such as time clocks); allow a reasonable amount of excused time for personal business (family affairs, meetings, and so on); and give the black the right to sign letters, reports, requisitions, and so on, as far as is consistent with his position.

Working conditions and facilities must be identical for all. Don't err by scrimping on offices or work space, meeting or conference rooms, or clerical aid for blacks. These deficiencies are inexcusable.

Individual treatment probably will prove to be the key to satisfying the black manager or professional. As his superior, you can give him that treatment by thoughtful consideration in matters such as these: Return his phone calls promptly. Allow him to see you as freely as possible; don't allow interruptions, especially phone calls, when he is seeing you. Give consideration to his individual work preferences, such as timing. Give him maximum participation in decision making and advance notice of changes. Always recognize good performance on his part.

The expectations and wants of the potential black manager or professional and the expectations and wants of the employer may be out of balance at the start. Thus *orientation*—the introduction of the Negro into your organization—usually proves decisive in determining whether he stays or leaves.

At one major company, young potential managers or professionals start out by reporting directly to a middle management supervisor and getting regular assignments immediately. On these, the newcomer must sink or swim, although the supervisor is close by in case of serious difficulty. But at this stage, the newcomer is allowed to make errors—according to the tried-and-true teaching maxim that a person learns more from his mistakes than his successes.

During their first year, all newcomers are evaluated on the basis of both their current job performance and their potential. If either assignment or performance indicates a need for a period of full-time training, they get it. However, this usually comes after the first year and is nearly always of a special nature—in data communication, for example—to tie in with a current assignment.

This approach has several notable features: The black employee receives immediate responsibility and so must sink or swim to some degree, but he also functions as an "intern" under a supervisor. In addition, specialized, formal, full-time training is provided to selected people to suit their needs, usually as required by a particular assignment.

When the day arrives for the first permanent job, you improve the chances that the Negro white-collar worker will stay with you if you start off on the right foot. Begin with a work-planning meeting; but, even before that session, tell the black employee what you plan to do, set a date for the meeting, prepare a work plan for him, provide at least one goal which will help him get the new knowledge or skill for his job, and review his total package. Then, at the work-planning session itself, you—

1. Discuss the plan with him thoroughly.
2. Review with him how you will work with him to plan his work and to review and recycle major goals.
3. Go through the plan goal by goal. Pinpoint the contributions each goal makes to overall plans. Show how it relates to the employee's responsibilities.
4. Go through the plan task by task. Show contribution of each task to the goal.
5. Set the date for your first review and recycling session—two weeks to one month later at most, depending on results and the employee's capability.

After the work-planning session, you should check yourself to see that you accomplished what you wanted. Then you should plan to visit the employee at his place of work to check on particular items and to get started on day-to-day coaching. You want to see, by an informal review of progress, whether he understands your expectations. Finally, you make it quite clear that he can expect decisions, information, and leadership from you.

Work planning is a process for individualizing business plans and for reviewing progress frequently in a problem-solving atmosphere. Its purpose is to clarify what the employee should do, to sustain interest in doing it, and to focus attention on better, more effective ways of doing it. All this should help keep him on the job.

The Special Problems

Special circumstances current in white-collar areas pose some problems that could lead to greater instability. Bernard Walker, as we noted, fears that the current climate of opinion, very much strengthened by the government's equal employment laws and procedures, will distort black people's views about the job situation in business and industry. This climate may even distort the actual job (it already has done so in some cases), making certain types of white-collar work "Negro positions." He cites jobs in "minority relations" or "urban affairs" as examples.

Charles Butler sees his major business problem as "trying to convince top management that a black man is capable of holding a non-showcase, top executive job."

Many of the people interviewed believe that the well-meaning federal regulations concerning equal employment do more harm than good. However, others believe they are necessary until "we get over the bridge—get accepted generally in business and industry." Howard Corey foresees greater job stability when Negroes are more at ease in managerial and professional positions, but he cautions that "black people must continue to get into influential positions if we are to make it."

John Chadwell sums it up: "Business and industry are now ready for us in managerial and professional jobs. It's up to us to meet the challenge."

PART SIX

Communicating

INTERVIEWS

Paul E. X. Brown

"All too frequently my white colleagues show no expression—no positive communication—toward me at all. But, on the other side of the coin, we must do some additional relating, too." That's how Paul E. X. Brown views the communication situation between the races. Brown, sales and marketing executive with the Atlanta Coca-Cola Bottling Company, has had a career typical of many middle-aged white-collar Negroes.

He was born in 1910 of middle-class parents and was graduated from the University of Minnesota in 1932. His parents had moved from Mississippi, where he had been born, to St. Louis. His father, now dead, was a successful schoolteacher and businessman.

Starting in 1942, Paul launched a career with Negro radio stations, including announcing, scriptwriting, and newscasting. He worked for stations in Chicago; Hammond, Indiana; Decatur, Georgia; Birmingham; and Atlanta. After a stint as program director for station WERD in Atlanta, he moved on to become editor-manager of the Georgia edition of the *Pittsburgh Courier,* a leading black newspaper. His journalism experience has also included a period as managing editor of *Negro Review,* a short-lived monthly news-pix pocket magazine.

Paul Brown applied for a job with the Atlanta Coca-Cola Bottling Company on the advice of the Urban League. He has moved into his present position after two years with the company. He says he hasn't "found the solution to opening up the gates for advancement."

With Coca-Cola Bottling, Brown is responsible for sales of services and products. He performs marketing studies and makes recommendations for marketing techniques. He is now executive director of the National Association of Market Developers, a society of black marketing professionals. Because of the scarcity of promotional opportunities, he hopes eventually to enter business as an owner or manager. If he were white, he believes, he would be earning 10 to 20 percent more than he is now and holding a more responsible position.

He and his wife have no children of their own, but he would definitely advise other youngsters to try for white-collar jobs in business and industry. "Break out of the present molds," he urges. "Stress to management your desires and ambitions. And get started as early as possible, because business has many facets."

A final word to youngsters from a man who has lived and worked for many years in Georgia: "The South holds many opportunities, and an ambitious black can achieve there."

Howard P. Corey

The present generation of young black adults (aged 25 to about 30) must "prime the pump" to get the Negro well started in managerial and professional jobs in business and industry, believes Howard Corey, who coordinates urban affairs activities for the Illinois Bell Telephone Company's suburban operations in the Chicago area.

Corey strongly urges young adults to sow the seeds for the generation coming up next, because "black people must continue to get into influential positions if we are to make it." He sees the fields of banking and investment as the prime job targets for the white-collar aspirant: "These are the areas black people must gain knowledge in if we are to survive." He recommends the West as the most promising geographical area—not so much because it is more hospitable than others to the Negro, but because it is growing fastest and will need more bright young managers and professionals.

Young black adults can "prime the pump" or "sow the seeds" by improving their communication with still younger people, "by spreading information about openings and advising high schools and colleges about what it takes to get a job."

Corey urges youngsters to "be black and understand what it means to be black." By this, he means that he believes Negroes follow a mistaken path if they try to be white Negroes. He wants youngsters to know and be proud of their black heritage, "get a good rounded education and never give up." He predicts that the path to the white-collar job will become progressively easier for Negroes for two reasons: first, pump priming now will make jobs flow more easily to black people in the years ahead; second, more white-collar jobs will exist—by 1975, about half of all jobs in the United States will be in this category.

Howard Corey points out that present white managers, from the standpoint of self-interest alone, if altruism and idealism don't motivate them, should actively recruit and promote blacks to make certain that enough managers and professionals will be around to run their companies in the years ahead. In short, he says to white managers: "Act more and don't let lip service alone pass for your contribution toward integrating the white-collar ranks."

Yet the pendulum shouldn't swing so far for white managers, cautions Corey, that they lose their objectivity. "Some blacks won't work out on white-collar jobs, just as some whites don't make the grade," he says. "Be fair and honest. Give sound constructive criticism when needed."

Corey was born in Cleveland, Mississippi, in 1940; his family moved to Chicago when he was young. His father now works in a steel-mill as a grinder, and his mother is employed as a packer in a bed factory. Corey went to Northwest Missouri State University, graduating in 1967 with a B.S. To help finance his education, he worked in the U.S. Post Office as a mail carrier and in a men's clothing store as a salesman. While in college, he applied for a job at Illinois Bell, and upon graduation he started as a facilities assistant. While progressing to his present job in urban affairs, he held the positions of traffic supervisor, assistant employee manager, and assistant staff supervisor. He hopes to move higher up in management, specializing in the areas of personnel and public relations.

His main problem in business: "Being thought of as an exceptional Negro because I have often been the first black person in a section." He resents being considered a freak on the one hand, but on the other hand he doesn't want constantly to be on guard against falling into the "tender trap" of thinking himself exceptional because patronizing whites imply he is. He has seen a few black colleagues almost ruin themselves because they came to half-believe they were "super." He guards against such pitfalls "by doing my thing—getting the job done."

Ellen Dammond

When asked, "What characteristics seem essential to the black manager or professional?" Mrs. Dammond answers:

1. Continued interest in advancement (with education to increase and expand one's interest in the world in which we live).
2. Ability to articulate goals, desires, and demands.
3. Willingness to assume responsibility and take risks in employment situations.
4. Curiosity and awareness of everything happening in the company, which can often affect employment opportunities.

She realizes that some of these characteristics are basically the same for whites. But in today's world, she feels, realistic blacks must be a bit more aggressive, try to develop a belief in themselves, and also possess a tough hide.

Mrs. Dammond obtained her A.B. degree from Bates College, in

Lewiston, Maine, in 1938. She did graduate work at the University of Pittsburgh and the New School for Social Research, New York. Over a span of 18 years, she has moved from the position of training supervisor to personnel counselor at B. Altman & Company, the New York department store.

Mrs. Dammond's sex has not hampered her in her career, she believes, because she has worked in an area traditionally open to women. However, her race has presented problems not normally confronted by a white person. She has attempted to solve such difficulties by meeting the issues head on, through open, honest discussion, to help enlighten management about situations with which it might be unfamiliar. For example, she makes the following suggestions:

1. Black speakers who understand the problems and issues of Negroes in business should speak to assembled groups of department managers and supervisors.
2. Courses that can improve blacks' knowledge of the business, or any business-related subject, should be offered or financed by employers.
3. Programs and seminars dealing with problems and issues in the black experience in business should be provided periodically.

Managers can better identify a potential manager or professional by making more effort to communicate with him, making frequent performance evaluations, and giving him the opportunity to carry more responsibility. For instance, Mrs. Dammond suggests that a candidate be tried out in more responsible jobs during vacation periods or through a system of rotating assignments. Such brief trial-and-error tours of duty will reveal much about a person's potential, she points out.

In some cases, Mrs. Dammond feels, managers should treat black white-collar employees differently from whites; for example, they should try to understand better the special frustrations and disappointments of Negroes. Managers should also do more to encourage blacks, while still insisting on good job performance. And managers seldom seek help often enough themselves in dealing with people with problems. Mrs. Dammond advises blacks to "increase managers' knowledge of the experience and frustrations of black people by suggesting courses, articles, books, and seminars for them to study."

What type of recruitment does Mrs. Dammond suggest? Seek black employees and promote long-time black employees from within. One way in which white managers can help blacks is to work to free themselves of attitudes which prevent promotions. This could be done by company programs, seminars, programs on human relations, and open black-white discussions. Mrs. Dammond says, "When whites seem limited in outlook, I try to help them broaden their outlook by using honesty and confrontation." The qualities she feels have been important to her in these endeavors are open-mindedness, a willingness to carry her share, a basically agreeable and optimistic nature, self-confidence, and enough humility to offset arrogance.

To sum it up, Ellen Dammond suggests to potential black managers and supervisors some means of preparation for such jobs: "Be well read; develop ability to articulate and write clear reports; stay abreast of the times; get further education if needed; take on new assignments as often as possible; and, last but not least, develop good basic work habits from the start."

Reginald L. Jones

Horatio Alger could have used Reg Jones's career as a scenario for one of his novels about the poor boy who gets ahead.

Dining-car waiter for five years on the Southern Pacific Railroad realizes he needs a college education. Gets one, winning B.S. in business administration at University of California in Berkeley at age 26, during depths of depression, in 1934. For seven years works for a Negro-owned and -managed insurance firm, Golden State Mutual Life Insurance Company. Has the title "salesman," but job includes collecting nickels, dimes, and quarters from his impoverished clients each week. To get more scope and pay, joins "white establishment," start-

186

ing as warehouseman and general clerk in 1941 with Lockheed Aircraft Corporation in Burbank, California. Having become a personnel representative (and moonlighting as coordinator of the Los Angeles Urban League's Industrial Relations Section), leaves Lockheed in 1948 to work for Los Angeles lumber firms, where he sells lumber and related supplies until 1961. Fails to marry boss's daughter, goes back to Lockheed, and is pretty well married to his job now.

Reg Jones was born in Monrovia, California, in 1908, the son of a railroader. He is a widower with one son, Robert, who also works for Lockheed. His son has been a factory transportation supervisor for seven years and is presently on a rotational management-development assignment while studying at Pepperdine College to obtain his M.B.A. under company sponsorship.

With the Lockheed-California Company, a division of Lockheed Aircraft Corporation, Jones is responsible for the dissemination of Plans for Progress and nondiscrimination policy throughout Lockheed. He contacts external organizations to provide information about Lockheed's merit employment policy and practice. He also keeps in touch with such organizations as the Urban League, churches, Negro fraternities, and schools and colleges to develop recruiting sources.

The nature of his work requires him to belong to many organizations, but fortunately he is, in his words, "a natural-born joiner." He remains active in the Los Angeles Urban League as a member of the board of directors. He is one of the associates of the Los Angeles City College; a member of the California Vocational Guidance Association; a member of the executive committee of the Los Angeles County Career Guidance Exhibits; a member of the board of directors of Dollars for Scholars, an organization to help needy students continue their education; a member of the Los Angeles City Schools Youth Motivation Task Force; a member of Men of Tomorrow, Inc.; and an alternate member of the Los Angeles Merit Employment Steering Committee. This last group is composed of more than 160 companies in the Los Angeles metropolitan area that have joined to promote equal employment.

Jones has the following suggestions for improving recruiting of minority-group people:

1. "Do more on-the-spot recruiting."

2. "Stop using the hackneyed phrase 'We are looking for qualified minority-group members but can't find them.'"
3. "Maintain a closer relationship with minority communities."

And Reg Jones offers these ideas to blacks themselves for getting good white-collar jobs and winning promotions in them: "Study, prepare, and continue to study. Your working life may span 45 years. Many changes can take place in your occupation or profession over that period of time."

He is not optimistic about the immediate future of black capitalism. "I see more and more," he says, "that 'white capitalism' is stifling black capitalism, perhaps inadvertently, by draining off the top qualified people into white businesses which can offer more money." Although he deplores this development, he believes that economic separatism of the races is neither possible nor desirable. "The ultimate goal," he believes, "is a fully integrated democracy where knowledge and know-how can be interchanged."

Jones suggests that a more complete interchange may come in the years ahead. Then the more experienced and capable Negroes may have more success with their own businesses. By that time, he hopes, such enterprises won't be tagged as "black capitalism" but, rather, looked on as "just companies that happen to be owned and managed by blacks."

Katheryn Emanuel Lawson

Mrs. Lawson makes the valid point that not all people—white or black—want white-collar jobs. Nor do all those—white or black—in the white-collar ranks aspire to high posts. "You can only really assist those who want the associated headaches of top-level positions," she cautions. Nevertheless, she believes that more Negroes are qualified to perform high professional and managerial work than actually do.

Present managers, says Mrs. Lawson, can identify such potential managers and professionals in the same way they identify white people for similar positions. She believes the common characteristic for any manager or professional, aside from expertise in his field, is "the ability to communicate to all levels—being able to say the right thing, at the right time, with the proper emphasis for effectiveness, whether the encounter is with the president of the corporation or the janitor." Yet the black person in managerial or professional work must possess additional qualities—"firmness with coworkers and avoidance of hypersensitivity (especially any which may be traceable to race problems)." And, to get ahead, she advises that ambitious blacks cultivate the "same hobbies and outside interests as the establishment."

As a staff member in physical science research for Sandia Laboratories in Albuquerque, New Mexico, the main problems which Katheryn Lawson faces in business that do not confront most of her white colleagues have to do with "special patronization." "I'm not sure that I solve these problems," she says. "Each instance has to be dealt with individually." Mrs. Lawson adds that not all such difficulties can really be "solved." She credits her "even disposition and willingness to recognize and accept human blunders for what they are" as the key to her ability to live with them. This does not mean that she ignores these problems, but her tactics for handling them are quite varied.

Mrs. Lawson advises white managers that the best way they can help Negroes to achieve promotions is "simply by not being afraid to recommend them." Black people can be better prepared for the office environment, especially in clerical and comparable levels, if they are "exposed to it, trained for it, and given jobs."

Mrs. Lawson was born Katheryn Emanuel in 1926 at Shreveport, Louisiana. Her mother is a retired elementary school teacher; her father, now dead, was a postman. She attended the public schools of Shreveport; received her A.B. from Dillard University in New Orleans in 1945, when she was only 18; and took her M.S. in chemistry at Tuskegee Institute in 1947. From 1947 to 1954, she held a series of college teaching jobs; during that period, she also did graduate work at the University of Wisconsin. She completed her studies at the University of New Mexico, obtaining her doctorate in 1957. She then took a position as biochemist at the Veterans Administration Hospital in Albuquerque. She joined Sandia Corporation in 1958, having applied directly for the position.

Katheryn Emanuel married Kenneth E. Lawson in 1954. Her husband was superintendent of the Albuquerque Sewer Division for 13 years, but since 1968 has served as assistant to the business manager of Southwestern Cooperative Education Laboratory, which devotes its efforts to adult basic education and training of culturally deprived children. The Lawsons have two sons, born in 1957 and 1959.

The Lawson family hopes to remain in Albuquerque. Katheryn Lawson, particularly, has sunk deep roots in the area. She is the newly elected vice-president of the Albuquerque Community Council and belongs to several other community and professional organizations. She is the author of many technical treatises connected with her scientific work at Sandia.

William G. Porter

"Improve your abilities in communication—oral and written." That's the advice of William G. Porter to black people who are potential members of the white-collar ranks and who want to prepare themselves for supervisory or management positions.

"I mean more than the ability to speak and write grammatically and clearly," he says. "I am concerned that the two races may polarize so drastically that they will end up completely unable to understand each other. Most Negroes of my generation have made a lifelong study of learning to communicate with whites. While many whites have unfortunately not reciprocated, members of the two races of about my age have achieved an understanding of sorts. But some younger blacks don't even try any longer to achieve understanding—to communicate. A white man may be careless or even contemptuous of learning to communicate with us, but that is no excuse or argument for the black man to repeat the same tragic mistake."

Bill Porter was born in 1909 in Montgomery, Alabama, the son of a postman and a schoolteacher. His education has included business college, American Management Association seminars, business courses for sales executives, and corporate seminars run by the University of Pennsylvania's Wharton School of Finance and Commerce. He has had more than 30 years of experience in sales with organizations ranging from a department store to a candy company to a Bible guild to a brewery. He has been with Anheuser-Busch, Inc., since 1952, rising up from the sales ranks to become assistant to the vice-president for marketing operations. His duties include sales promotion planning; special market policy making; planning and conducting meetings with wholesalers, sales representatives, and the news media; market surveying; and development of corporate community participation at the national level.

Bill Porter describes the difficulties he faces in a predominantly white business establishment as "socioeconomic problems." He solves them through "tact, persistence, and experience."

Essential to the Negro or white manager or professional, he feels, are "training, social intelligence, and a willingness to learn, plus freedom from race psychology." These qualities are essential to everyone who aspires to managerial or professional positions.

Mr. Porter urges "greater dedication to duty on the part of minority-group personnel as a road to the top." He sees the current disenchantment with the white business establishment by some young people—mostly white—as an opportunity for black young people to step in and show what they can do. "Now is an ideal time for Negro youngsters," he points out. An acute shortage of qualified management personnel means that business and industry must recruit the black man to help run the organization. Present management "will place our young men with potential in growth positions," he says.

Of course, this bright potential could be dimmed, he acknowledges, if the races polarize even more than they already have. "The whites need us, but we need the whites," he explains. To reduce the polarization, he urges "imagination, diplomacy, and a positive attitude toward life." He believes that Negroes will have a progressively easier time in white-collar jobs as more and more achieve them. Right now, black people need more examples of success in managerial and professional positions which they can emulate.

For the time being, Bill Porter feels, it is necessary "to prime the pump by placing more young Negroes in positions with growth potential." Beyond that, it is the responsibility of the individual to further his qualifications for advancement through enrollment in special courses.

Mr. and Mrs. Porter are the parents of three grown children, two daughters and a son. Their son is with the St. Louis Human Development Corporation as a program-development specialist.

William Snoddy

Better communication—black to black, black to white, and white to black—is one of the prescriptions offered by William Snoddy to increase the number of Negroes in managerial and professional positions in business and industry.

Snoddy, a materials engineer with American Airlines, points out that Negroes themselves need to do a better job of informing their fellows of the availability and attractions of white-collar work. To accomplish this, he suggests the following steps:

- Spread the word at church meetings, social affairs, and the like about white-collar opportunities. Black leaders in key positions in the community, particularly, should keep Negroes informed of job opportunities.
- Take an active part in community politics. This is one of the best ways to tune in on the local grapevine.
- Do your best on your own job, accepting ever increasing responsibilities. The "living witness" is the oldest and best form of advertising.

Bill Snoddy believes that, when more Negroes attain white-collar positions, the job of communicating about them will be almost self-perpetuating. But, until blacks become commonplace in such work, "pump priming" must continue.

As far as black-to-white communication is concerned, he tries "to improve it between management and myself, to show or prove that I am a man with constructive ideas, principles, and good business sense." He offers these suggestions on how to improve black-to-white communication:

- "I let the boss know my thoughts, including both criticism and praise, about the business."
- "I let him know that I know my job. Nothing attracts confidence and respect more quickly than demonstrated knowledge."
- "I show as often as possible that I'm willing to accept responsibilities."
- "Finally, I demonstrate that I can handle added responsibilities."

White-to-black communication also needs improvement, Bill Snoddy thinks. He suggests to white colleagues that they let the Negro know that he is needed, wanted, and expected to do the job; let him know when he is doing a good or bad job; and translate the communication into action by promoting, retraining, transferring, or even discharging when appropriate.

Snoddy especially emphasizes the need to couple action with communication. For one thing, he points to the problem of compensation. "I believe blacks generally are on the low side of the salary scale," he says. "White management always gives the impression that things will be better in the future. Yet the action is slow in coming." He cites other inconsistencies between action and communication— for example, in promotions and in words about equality that contrast with actions indicating condescension.

Bill Snoddy acknowledges, however, that "things are changing and changing for the better for Negroes." More white managers and professionals than formerly, he points out, are willing "to give their black colleagues an opportunity to prove they can do a good job." Negroes enjoy more job autonomy and responsibility than in the past, he believes.

He would advise his three young sons and his daughter to aspire to white-collar work in business and industry when they grow up, "because this is the big new field opening up to blacks." He would suggest that they set their sights on the work that interests them. However, he will insist that they get an education "to be properly qualified when the opportunity comes along." Hurting the cause now, he points out, are those people, especially in technically oriented fields, "who can't live up to the expectations and standards of the job."

Bill Snoddy holds a B.S. from Langston University in Oklahoma. He was born in 1937 in Fort Worth, Texas. His father is dead, and his mother is now married to a clergyman. After college, Bill worked for the G. T. Grant Company as a stockroom manager. He joined North American Aviation in Tulsa, Oklahoma, in September 1963 as a research analyst. Then, in April 1967, he moved over to American Airlines in Tulsa by walking into the employment office, filling out an application, and asking for the job.

As a materials engineer, Snoddy is responsible for projects associated with a wide variety of plastic and bonded materials that go into aircraft. He hopes eventually to better his present position by becoming manager of one of American's technical departments.

James Stewart

"The problems concerning blacks in private industries are white problems. It's about time the whites went through some of the changes, rather than sending us through them all." So says James Stewart, a purchasing agent with the Kaiser Aluminum & Chemical Company in New Orleans. And he has other plain-spoken advice to whites.

"There's no real problem finding qualified blacks. The problem is that you are looking for blacks who might fit your white image. Stop feeling as though you're doing us a favor by letting us work with you. Stop letting your ignorance of the black man get in the way of judging us as individuals. Stop your condescension; stop feeling superior solely because you're white and we're black. Quit worrying about how other whites will feel about blacks being promoted."

To his fellow Negroes, he says: "Don't sell your blackness for a job. Help other blacks win white-collar positions by putting in a good word for them and by giving them tips you have learned from your experience with white management. Don't be afraid to speak up to white management. Urge them to make a commitment to hire more of us in managerial and professional positions."

Jim Stewart believes communication between the races needs substantial improvement. "We're not getting across to each other," he feels. "The whites act as though there's a stigma on us. We react accordingly. But the burden's on the whites to forget that myth of the stigma." The mythical stigma, he feels, limits where a white employer will send a black man in the nation, how far he'll promote him, and even the kind of job he'll give him.

Stewart was born in Oakland, California, on January 3, 1945. He received his B.A. from Fresno State College, California, in 1967. His father is a minister and his mother a school clerk. Stewart was a teacher for a while, after trying his luck as a professional football player in the Continental League as a flanker back. He decided to leave the game after a knee injury which necessitated a series of operations.

With Kaiser, he's in charge of all electrical and electronics purchasing for the corporation's southern regional purchasing department. This includes five domestic and three foreign plants. His goal is to become the head purchasing agent at a plant. For the long term, he wants to become a plant manager or corporate executive.

Jim Stewart has no children and is not sure he would advise a son or daughter to try for a white-collar job in business or industry. "Crafts and trade seem to provide more security and often pay more money. I'd tell them to evaluate all areas in accordance with their capabilities, but not to be afraid to try anything."

He is married to Faye Stewart, presently an art-education major at Southern University, New Orleans.

James I. Walton

"Being black, I felt that I would be faced with difficult problems in getting subordinate whites to work for me. To my surprise, that hasn't been true."

That has been the experience of James I. Walton, a personnel manager with Honeywell, Inc. He attributes this result to his "ability to meet, be friendly, and communicate with people regardless of their status in the organization. I feel that I am aggressive yet tactful and have the ability to adjust to changes and circumstances." He adds: "We are all human beings with our individual differences. It is my belief and experience that you must deal with each person separately, regardless of race. If you treat others with respect, you will receive the same.

"The black man isn't really asking for any special treatment," Walton says. "He merely wants a real chance to demonstrate his own competence and ability." While Walton does not think managers should treat black white-collar employees differently from whites, he acknowledges that there are some special circumstances "where the manager will have to spend additional efforts to get blacks to become productive employees." He cites cases such as these as examples of situations where special treatment is justified.

1. Sometimes the new black employee will not be able to meet the work standards that have been set up, predicated on white production standards, because he will experience additional initial job pressures which whites seldom encounter (differences in language and so on). "When these differences appear, the manager will have to work with and be more lenient with the black," says Walton.
2. "When a black person is the first of his race in the department where the work flow is heavily influenced by teamwork," Wal-

ton says, "the manager may have a difficult time getting this employee adjusted to his work environment—particularly if some of the team members are a nest of prejudiced whites."

3. "When a black is relocated to a new location where he runs into trouble finding adequate housing," Walton warns, "management must extend itself to insure that the employee gets settled in a desirable area as soon as possible."

4. And Jim Walton believes that an effort should often be made to insure that communication is better with the new black employee than with whites. "Black people often have mistaken expectations about promotion," he says. "They tend to expect too much or too little. The manager should explain the realities of promotion." He adds: "Many blacks don't know the procedure for applying for promotions. This should be carefully communicated."

Walton suggests the following types of recruiting to move more black employees into white-collar jobs: "Recruit at the college level in predominantly black colleges. Recruit through employment agencies specializing in black employment. Provide summer employment for students between junior and senior years or between graduate years. Make such work meaningful, not just a routine or 'showcase' job."

He advises blacks who are potential members of the white-collar ranks and who aspire to supervisory positions "to take advantage of the special seminars and courses offered through many companies, to use tuition-aid programs and courses through the American Management Association and other organizations, and to keep up on business reading—books, magazines, and newspapers."

Present managers—white and black—can better prepare Negroes for the office environment by being concerned themselves, by counseling students to take proper preparatory courses, and by urging them to attend special training programs. Walton points out that blacks are no different from whites when it comes to movitation. "Expose them," he says, "to better-paying, more meaningful and responsible positions." He adds that "having blacks in high-level management jobs within the organization proves especially helpful."

Jim Walton follows his own advice on advancement. He aims at the next-highest level in his profession—a personnel director of one of Honeywell's divisions. His long-range plan is to become a vice-president of employee relations with Honeywell or another top company. He's taking advantage of the many seminars conducted by AMA, the University of Michigan's Industrial Center, and Honeywell itself, and he is also enrolled in the University of Minnesota's evening school, preparing for a master's degree in industrial relations.

Walton was born in September 1935 in Macon, Georgia, but his family moved to St. Paul, Minnesota, when he was young. His father is a civilian employed with the U.S. Air Force as a senior clerk, and his mother is an assembler in a small box factory. Walton went through the St. Paul public school system and then entered Iowa State University in Ames, where he took his B.S. in industrial relations. He helped finance his college education by working during summers as a dining-car waiter. In the military, he served as a schoolteacher, helping school dropouts in the service obtain their high school equivalency diplomas. From 1962 to 1964 he worked for the Minnesota State Employment Service as a labor-market analyst. He joined Honeywell as a compensation analyst in 1964; in 1966, the company promoted him to his personnel managership in the field-marketing organization of the corporate staff.

Jim Walton and his wife have one son, born in February 1967. Would Walton advise his son to enter business when he grows up? Here is how he answers that question: "Even after four years of employment at Honeywell, I still find a few managers reluctant to accept me for what I can do. But, overall, I can say that my acceptance has been great. By the time my son grows up, I believe that blacks in industry will be much more commonplace than now. The road won't be smooth, however. Everyone in business, white or black, must always set ever higher standards for himself—even higher than his boss sets for him. Racial prejudice will remain, I fear, when my son grows up, but I will still advise him to go into business if he wishes. Yet he should embark on such a career with his mind open, not empty—ready for racial rebuff but not overly concerned about those individuals who don't really accept you as a colleague or manager."

DISCUSSION

"I've recently hired two hard-core people," a manager told a friend.

Unfortunately, the two new employees overheard him. One had an M.B.A. and the other a B.S. in electrical engineering. Both had more education than the manager, and one came from an economic background more affluent than the manager's. However, the two new employees were black, and the manager was white.

This episode illustrates how the careless use of words—poor communication—poses a formidable barrier to good black-white relationships in the white-collar ranks of business and industry. Actually, the National Alliance of Businessmen describes the typical "hard-core" trainee as someone who has been unemployed for at least 18 months, who has no intensive skilled training, whose parents are unskilled; who has had little experience with doctors and needs eyeglasses and dental help right away, who lacks transportation facilities, who has no education beyond the sixth grade, who lives with one and a half families, who has had scrapes with the law which resulted in at least 30 days in jail, and who is married and has had three children. The two new bachelor employees in no way matched that profile; both required eyeglasses, it's true, but they already had them.

Katheryn Lawson points out that the important common-denominator characteristic required for any manager or professional, aside from expertise in his field, is "the ability to communicate to all levels —being able to say the right thing, at the right time, with the proper emphasis for effectiveness, whether the encounter is with the president or the janitor of the corporation."

Three Communication Axioms

The thoughtless remark about "hard-core people" suggests three axioms about interpersonal communication.

1. Everything you do or don't do, say or don't say, communicates something. It is impossible not to communicate. The manager's attitude toward the two newcomers, obviously, was

condescending. It probably would have shown in his actions or attitudes even if he had never made the derogatory remark.

2. Because you communicate in everything you do or say, you must take care to do and say everything as positively as possible.

3. Whoever communicates the most effectively will generate the action. One of the young employees resigned within six months. The "hard core" comment proved just the beginning of a series of communications, most of them subliminal, that prompted his departure. The manager's communication did not precipitate positive action, but it did lead to action.

Negative communication is a serious problem when it occurs, but a far more common communication fault among American white businessmen in dealing with blacks is the absence of positive communication. Because most white-dominated companies have for generations virtually ignored Negroes as white-collar employees, their managements have communicated to the black community that business and industry has little interest in them as managers or professionals. It's no wonder that many blacks are not yet certain that management really wants them in the white-collar sector. That's the message communicated by a couple of centuries of near silence on the matter.

Yet many white managers today profess puzzlement over black skepticism about the intentions of the "establishment." "I have never once in my life said I wouldn't hire a qualified Negro!" exclaimed one businessman. But he never said that he would, either. Just silence.

The Problem of Isolation

"All too frequently," says Paul Brown, "my white colleagues show no expression—no positive communication—toward me at all. But, on the other side of the coin, we must do some additional relating, too." This sort of isolation probably poses the gravest danger to communication between the races. Bill Porter puts it this way: "I am concerned that the two races may polarize so drastically that they will end up completely unable to understand each other."

This problem extends even beyond race. Many managers—white

and black—think that communication is an isolated part of their job. Yet communication is like the cloth in your suit, not the mere button on your sleeve. Just as the cloth determines the shape, texture, and quality of the garment, communication determines the shape, texture, and quality of your performance. The better the cloth, the better the suit. The better your communication, the better your performance.

Apart from racial barriers to business communication, another problem is the tendency to make communication largely of the old factory sort—"Tell them, don't talk to them." This kind of communication probably doesn't even work well in the factory any more, because employees are too well educated and too sophisticated to stand for it. But the approach certainly fails utterly with the white-collar class now growing in numbers and importance in industry.

The Problem of Complacency

Jim Stewart complains: "We're not getting across to each other. The whites act as though there's a stigma on us. We react accordingly." Indeed, there is no doubt that the complacent feeling of superiority to blacks that many whites still hold obviously is a barrier to good communication between the races.

But, apart from racial complacency, there is a more fundamental aspect of this same fault: We have all been talking and listening for so long that we tend to think we're experts. One manager expressed surprise when he learned about the ineffectiveness of his communication. "Why, I've been talking practically all my life," he protested. "If those guys don't understand me, they'd better remove their earplugs."

We all must bring ourselves up short from time to time and not take our ability to communicate for granted.

The Problem of Superficiality

Still another problem handicaps communication between people —superficiality. Some managers appear to believe they are "communicating" if they address employees by their first names and smile continually. When joviality goes no further than that, it means as much as the average receptionist's smile. If you think you are communicating effectively because you use these tactics, take care.

In his book *Memoirs of Childhood and Youth,* the noted philosopher and humanitarian Albert Schweitzer said: "We wander through life together in a semidarkness in which none of us can distinguish exactly the features of his neighbor; only from time to time, through some experience that we have of our companion, or through some remark that he passes, he stands for a moment clear to us, as though illuminated by a flash of lightning."

We don't advocate omitting the social lubricants—first names, inquiries after health—but we are deluding ourselves when we mistake these for the "flash of lightning." We need genuine flashes, and one way to get them is by paying more attention to personal communication. Are we doing this? Aaron Levenstein doesn't think so; in his book *Why People Work,* he says: "With all the progress we have made, with planes and radio and television, the speed or efficiency of personal communication on which business organizations depend internally has not increased appreciably."

We need the greater efficiency of communications to keep pace with the ever quickening rate of change in our economy. We should communicate effectively so as to enable our people to welcome, not fear, the most certain development they will encounter in their working lives—change.

Mass Communication and the Time Problem

Superficiality leads to another communication problem—we "mass communicate" too much. We tend to believe that the employee publication will solve all our communication problems or even that a notice on the bulletin board will do the job. Under these conditions, communication becomes impersonal rather than interpersonal, so that we lose one of the great advantages of oral communication— the intimacy of face-to-face talk. Such a relationship is a basic human need, providing warmth in a business relationship that so easily can get cold.

And then there is the lack of time from which so many of us suffer. Clarence B. Randall, late chairman of Inland Steel Company, had a word about this: "Gone from our lives today are those periods of intellectual and spiritual pause for reflection which made our forebears strong. Each day we are engulfed by the chaos and confusion which surround us. Sober thought before decision taking is difficult to achieve. We tend instead to guide our lives by intuitive reactions, often those which are induced by external forces of which we are but dimly aware."

One of those external forces is no longer so obscure. It's race. In the hurly-burly of business today, just because we are pressed for time, we often allow our racial prejudices to dictate how we communicate.

The Words of Speech

Webster defines "communication" as an act or instance of transmitting, information communicated, a verbal or written message, an exchange of information, a process by which meanings are exchanged between individuals through a common system of symbols, a technique for expressing ideas effectively in speech or writing. Communication, then, is a word that can mean many things. Ever since man started using symbols and sign language, he has had problems of communicating with others. There can be a communication gap between age groups of the same race, between technical and non-technical people, between management and labor—and, of course, between white managers and black employees.

For the moment, let's consider that last communication gap. Here are some examples:

- If a black tells a young black white-collar worker "Work hard; get a good education, because you really need it," this can be understood in at least two different ways. A white person overhearing it may think, "All blacks need special training and education to bring them up to entry-level white-collar standards." But the black aspirant hears, "Be better than average. You must excel because the white business will not accept, hire, or let you get ahead otherwise."
- When a top manager says, "Let's prime the pump to help the

Negroes," some blacks may think he means, "He'll give one or two showcase jobs." But others—not nearly as many—may interpret the remark to mean, "He will make a conscientious effort to find, hire, promote, and put blacks in good jobs with a future."

■ Or take the varying connotations of "black power." In some quarters, this brings to mind a bearded black militant with a raised fist and a gun in the other hand. Most blacks, however, think of black power as the solidification of black communities toward the goal of political and economic power.

Yet there's plenty of trouble with communicating even without race. Most people are wrong if they think they can understand each other simply because they both speak English. In one case, an intelligent and well-educated Frenchman caused mild concern at a polite New York party when he used the term "half-fast," referring to a somewhat lackadaisical colleague. He had heard the term among his English-speaking friends, but he had never seen it in print and assumed it was spelled as it appears here and meant "desultory." His friends later had to explain to him that it was actually spelled "half-assed" and did not precisely mean what he had thought.

Similarly, a Northerner in an advertising agency used the expression "call a spade a spade" in his copy for an ad. A Southerner had to explain that the expression was not the happiest choice for the South, where the ad was scheduled to appear widely, because "spade" is an opprobrious term for a Negro.

Words failed in these instances. Students of language would explain that the examples illustrate difficulties in semantics, which is "the study of the meanings of speech forms, especially of the development and changes in meaning of words and word groups."

Many explanations account for such confusions as we have noted. For example, take the vagaries of English. The 500 most common English words have more than 14,000 meanings as listed in *The Concise Oxford Dictionary*—and these include just the normally accepted meanings, not the specialized and emotional definitions that are attached to words like "integrate," "bussing," and a host of others.

Semantic problems also crop up in "multivalued" words. "Through" and "threw" sound alike, for instance. There's no trouble

204

with them in print, but context must rule in oral communication. Other familiar homonyms are "fair" and "fare"; "read" and "reed"; "four," "for," and "fore"; and "to," "too," and "two."

Homographs also lead to confusion. These are words with the same spelling and often the same pronunciation, but with a different meaning. Examples: "bass" for a fish and a man's voice; "lead" as "to direct" and as a metal.

On another level, we must consider meanings as influenced by personal associations. "Black" is an obvious example. "Black is beautiful" to Negroes, but it is simply one of the colors to many white people and a racist expression to others.

Still another problem with language is its slippery quality—it won't stand still either in time or in place. Francis Bacon described people as "indifferent, obnoxious, and officious." In his day that meant "impartial, submissive, and ready to serve." And geography has an effect on language. "To table" in England means "to put something on the table for immediate consideration." In America, it means "to put aside for later consideration."

While these idiosyncrasies of language prove troublesome, they fade to only minor concerns when we consider such subtler problems as these:

1. *Turning ordinary words into "color" words.* "Black" is a prime example, but there are many others—"integrate," "communist," "hippie," and so on.

2. *Confusing facts with inferences and opinions.* A supervisor wanted to fire a Negro employee because he was "never on time." Investigation by the personnel department turned up the fact that the employee had been late twice in the previous month. It also turned up the fact that the supervisor currently had only the one black employee and that blacks previously placed in his department had all left for one reason or another. This superintendent was confusing inferences with facts and thereby rationalizing his racial bias. The personnel manager had several lengthy sessions with the man in an effort to persuade him to mend his ways.

3. *Expressing everything in extreme terms.* Words like "good" or "bad," "right" or "wrong," "clean" or "dirty" are clear-cut words. We tend to use them rather than the less dramatic "fairly good" or "partly right," which actually may be more precise statements of a situation. Because we don't want to bother to find the precise term, we often

carelessly pick the extreme term. Usually this practice does no serious harm—but consider its effect when we are appraising a man's promotability or deciding whether he deserves a salary adjustment.

4. *Identifying falsely on the basis of words.* The following story illustrates this point: A policeman ordered student demonstrators to move away from the college president's office. "We don't want any trouble with you reds," he told one placard-carrying picketer. "I'm anticommunist," replied a bearded Negro. "I don't care what kind of a communist you are," the policeman insisted. "Move along."

A common difficulty with false identification in business dealings with blacks occurs when management assumes that Negro employees agree with its position on a particular issue only to find that the opposite is the case. This happened when one company's black recruiting program failed dismally. The recruiting manager called in a Negro employee and asked, "What do you think happened? You agreed that it was a good approach." The black had to deny that he thought the approach sensible. "I never said it was," he pointed out. "You showed it to me and others when it was all ready to go. We didn't think we could point out at that late stage that we thought the psychology bad. Besides, we thought maybe we were wrong. None of us has had much experience with recruiting. You have."

Most blacks are not yet accustomed to contradicting whites, despite the noise from the militants among them. A white manager must learn to draw out any negative opinions from them with patience and understanding.

5. *Using "businessese."* "Governmentese" has its counterpart in industry. Examples of business jargon:

"Let's have your input on this." (Translation: "Please cooperate more.")

"We need your report update." (Translation: "Your report's late. Get it in now.")

"Do this job soonest." (Translation: "Do it immediately, if not yesterday.")

The jargon user always wants to be current; and, in order to be current with black employees, white managers have even been heard using what they think is "jive" talk—"Hey, man!" "Slip me some skin." Or: "You're hip." This sort of thing should be avoided.

6. *Using general abstractions.* "They want you to get this job out by 5 o'clock," said the manager of the drafting department. Who's

"they"? It's far more effective to say, "President Smith wants this job out by 5 o'clock." Or even, "The customer wants this job out .by 5 o'clock."

The thoughtless use of general abstractions is inexcusable but nevertheless common. When they are more subtle than the example given, they can cause real trouble. "Black power," for example, is so abstract and general that it's nearly meaningless; but, we have already seen, it and other terms easily become color words. Phrases including the word "big" are particularly dangerous in this respect: "Big Labor, Big Business." And think of the implications of Wall Street!

Yet this doesn't mean that you should never use specific abstractions. Einstein formulated his theory of relativity by thinking abstractly—but specifically. In fact, man has made his greatest intellectual strides when dealing in abstractions, then putting the generalizations into concrete form.

Don't use abstractions carelessly. Don't use them at all when a more specific description is available.

Three Other Communication Barriers

If race and semantics were the only barriers to effective communication, we would have trouble enough, but at least three more plague us in our attempt to get across to others. They are shortcomings in our communication content, shortcomings in our communication strategy, and difficulties associated with listening.

Content. The most common shortcoming in communication content is a lack of goals. In communication between the races in business, the goal too often appears to be to get it accomplished with a minimum of fuss. The result frequently is an abrupt, impersonal performance; incomplete information is transmitted, and the listener's intelligence is underestimated and his fund of knowledge overestimated.

When your communication content is inadequate, take these steps to correct the fault:

1. Take your time.

2. Never underestimate the listener's intelligence.
3. Never overestimate his fund of knowledge.
4. Know your goals in communicating—to motivate as well as to inform.
5. Communicate the higher purposes and meaning of the job.
6. Give full and accurate information.
7. Know your facts; don't guess or fake.
8. Know the real problems facing you. Beware of reading too much or too little into situations that confront you.

Strategy. Another major barrier to communication is poor strategy. The most common error here lies in the communicator's belief that the listener eagerly awaits his message. Substitute "resignedly" for "eagerly" and you will come closer to the truth. Another strategic difficulty arises, especially between the races, in the poor image that a communicator may project, usually inadvertently. Louise Prothro points to this common strategic error by whites: "The naïve questions raised by white associates when the black question comes up are unthinkable."

A further consideration is the receiver of your communication. Do you know him? How do you handle a situation in which he disagrees with you? Do you work with, not on, him? Do you know—and face—the true issue?

When your communication strategy is under par, you can improve it if you will—

1. Expect resistance.
2. Project your best image.
3. Know your receiver and put the message into his context.
4. Develop a feedback system to check on how you are getting across.
5. Use disagreement creatively, perhaps to develop a course of action better than the one you had first considered.
6. Work with, rather than on, people.
7. Know, face, and deal with the true issue.

Listening. Yet another communication barrier develops because most of us are poor listeners. The average manager spends about 80 percent of his time communicating. A great proportion of that time —45 percent of it—is spent listening.

Many factors contribute to difficulties with listening, but these stand out:

1. *Inadequate background information.* Most listeners don't want to admit they lack information; so ignorance and pride result in a listening failure.
2. *Selective inattention.* We hear what we want to hear.
3. *Selective memory.* We remember what we want to remember, usually the good news, the compliments, or the readily understood bits of information.
4. *Selective expectation.* We all tend to anticipate what someone will say. If he doesn't speak according to our anticipated script, we may not hear the detour.
5. *Bias.* This goes beyond race. Simply because we do not like the communicator we may not listen fully to what he says.
6. *Resistance to influence.* This is a step down from bias and even more common. People don't want their opinions changed, even if the opinions prove wrong.
7. *Boredom.* Communicate in as lively a manner as possible, if only to surmount this obstacle. If you find your attention wandering, take stern measures with yourself. For the listener, self-discipline is the principal antidote to boredom.
8. *Partial listening.* Many of us hear the words but don't see the facial expressions that may transmit at least half the message.

To overcome these problems always pay attention to acoustics, physical comfort, and timing in communications with employees. If possible, insist on a quiet place and comfortable surroundings. See that there are no interruptions, and choose a time when the entire message can be heard.

And improve your emotions for better listening—especially to overcome selective inattention, selective memory, selective expectation, bias, fear of being influenced, and boredom. Listening is vastly improved if you have empathy toward the speaker. Be alert when you listen—don't slouch, and look directly at the speaker. Never flatly contradict him.

Still another way to improve your listening is to refrain from talking so much yourself. To know whether you err in this respect, ask yourself these questions:

1. Do I explain my own position in excessive detail?
2. Do I plan answers while the other person is still talking?
3. Do I often get impatient while others are talking?
4. Do I often miss another's point?

If you must answer yes to just one of those questions, you probably have a mild case of verbosity. The treatment you should take includes the following steps:

1. *Confine yourself to asking questions.* Remain silent for five seconds, at least, after each one.
2. *Force yourself to listen.* Time your silences.
3. *Let the other listeners, if any, answer questions or respond to the speaker.* If you are the only listener, reply briefly.
4. *Practice brevity* in all your remarks.

The Communication Basics

To summarize, these are the basics of good communication:

1. *Know your audience.* This would appear obvious, but many people overlook the obvious. Nearly all the people interviewed urge whites to know blacks better. A few also suggest the reverse—that blacks should know whites better.

2. *Build on the past.* Start with what the audience already knows. Louise Prothro complains of the "contrived ignorance" of many whites. For instance, some whites communicate as though they are unaware of blacks' problems with housing.

3. *Know your purpose.* Keep your objectives always in mind. Do more than tell your audience what to do—motivate them to do it better than they have ever done it before.

4. *Think and organize.* The old axiom "Look before you leap" applies here. It is better to say nothing than to say something unwise. It is better, also, to say nothing than to be so wordy and disjointed that your people can't make anything out of what you say or—much worse—interpret it wrongly.

5. *Emphasize the positive.* Tell your listeners what they are doing right. Of course, you must correct errors, but do it positively by using the proper approach. Watch, particularly, the "negative-prone" em-

ployees—the ones who get easily discouraged or who have a tendency toward low spirits and pessimism. Save up bits of good news for them. Go easy on the criticism.

6. *Do not eliminate the negative.* When bad news does turn up, do not gloss over it or suppress it. Bad news always comes out, usually more quickly than good news. You gain tactical advantages when you give it in your own way and at your own time. But never exaggerate bad news. (Some people tend to do so.)

7. *Guard your credibility.* Your reputation for honesty and objectivity is difficult to develop and easy to lose. And it is your most valuable asset. Blacks are particularly sensitive to whites' credibility; so whites should take particular pains in this area.

8. *Act on what you say.* This builds credibility. Nearly every black has experienced the job interview in which the position mysteriously disappears when the employer learns the applicant's race. Reg Jones adds: "Stop using the hackneyed phrase, 'We're looking for qualified minority-group people but can't find them.' "

9. *Keep your emotional content up.* Many people who do not know the business world well equate industry with an unemotional matter-of-factness. Yet neither matter-of-factness nor lack of emotion is characteristic of an effective organization. Rather, it is an exciting, stimulating, challenging place to work. Emotions, within reason, are given full play. Emotionalism comes from a deep understanding of mutual purpose and from a strong desire to do better—both of which are, indeed, common to management at its best. Moreover, they are and should be expressed with eloquence—the sort of eloquence that goes to the heart because it reveals the heart of a situation and that comes naturally with a clear purpose and strong desire. John Walker may have had this in mind when he said an aspirant for a management position must "have the gift of gab."

10. *Give the full picture.* Partial communication is unsuccessful communication. James Walton points out what can happen when explanations about advancement opportunities are poor. "Black people often have mistaken expectations about promotion," he says. "They tend to expect too much or too little. The manager should explain the realities of promotion. Many don't know the procedure for applying for promotions. This should be carefully communicated."

11. *Pay attention to nonverbal aspects of communicating.* Ac-

tions speak louder than words, and so may facial expressions and gestures. Don't let inadvertent grimaces or gestures belie the intended meaning of your words.

12. *Communicate a little at a time.* Don't give a long message in one indigestible gulp. Try to space out complicated communication into digestible pieces.

13. *Give a story in a variety of ways.* This is a corollary of the "bit by bit" maxim. Since you usually must repeat your story, use a variety of presentations.

14. *Know your communicating score.* The best gauge is the overall job your people do. One approach: Win such high confidence and respect from your audience that it will tell you how you are coming through. Let your people know you want their reaction. And, when you have an effective feedback system, pay attention to it. Listen.

Black-to-Black Communication

Until recently, Negro professionals and managers communicated very little with their less fortunate "brothers." But black awareness has generated a desire to pull together. Here are a few of the areas in which efforts are increasing:

- Encouraging young Negroes to go into industry. Howard Corey advises his associates "to spread information about openings and to advise high schools and colleges about what it takes to get a job."
- Explaining the requirements and qualifications needed for particular positions. Says Harvey Brewster: "Black people can help Negroes win promotions by explaining how to avoid various job-related obstacles as white-collar workers."
- Explaining to black neophytes about company policies and so on.
- Expanding arrangements like the Big Brother Organization, which is devoted to self-help for black employees.

Some 80 percent of those interviewed said they would definitely advise their young children to try for managerial or professional careers in business when they grow up. As the communication of those ideas spreads throughout the black communities, the supply of applicants will increase.

Some Negroes feel that black awareness may swing too far. Ted Nims sums it up this way: "It isn't necessary for us to wear Afro dress to be identified as black. Wear such styles if you like them, but for no other reason. The whites already know that we're black."

The theme running throughout the responses is the message of blacks to other blacks: "Be yourself; be ready (educationally); excel on the job."

Black-to-White and White-to-Black Communication

Concerning the improvement of black-to-white communication, Bill Snoddy echoes the beliefs of many. He says that he tries "to improve it between management and myself, to show or prove that I am a man with constructive ideas, principles, and good business sense." He offers these suggestions:

- "I let the boss know my thoughts, including both criticisms and praise."
- "I let him know that I know my job."
- "I show that I'm willing to accept responsibilities."
- "I demonstrate that I can handle added responsibilities."

White-to-black communication also needs improvement, he thinks. He suggests to white colleagues that they let the Negro know that he is needed, wanted, and expected to do a job; let him know when he is doing a good or bad job; and translate the communication into action by promoting, retraining, transferring, or even discharging when appropriate.

Bill Snoddy especially emphasizes the need for whites to couple action with communication. For example, he points to the problem of compensation. "I believe blacks generally are on the low side of the salary scale," he says. "White managements always give the impression that things will be better in the future. Yet the action is slow in coming."

Suggestions for white managers and professionals to help keep the channels open include these do's and don'ts.

DON'T—

- Use phrases like "Some of my best friends are . . . ," "I've had some tough days in my time . . . ," "I understand how you feel . . . ," "Hey, you . . . ," "Say, Junior . . . ," "Hey, boy. . . ."
- Allow or tell racial jokes.
- Treat or regard interactions between minority-group members any differently than interactions between minority-group members and others.
- Philosophize on racial issues with blacks.
- Allow condescending attitudes toward black colleagues.
- Assume that you have no racial prejudices—that the other fellow is to blame.

DO—

- Insure that minority-group members get full training.
- Give career guidance.
- Provide upgrading activities.
- Provide opportunities for day-to-day contact with whites.

Bill Porter sums it up this way: "Improve your abilities to communicate—oral and written. I mean more than the ability to speak and write grammatically. . . . Most Negroes of my generation have made a lifelong study of learning to communicate with whites. While many whites have unfortunately not reciprocated, members of the two races of about my age have achieved understanding of sorts. But some younger blacks don't even try any longer to achieve understanding—to communicate. A white man may be careless or even contemptuous of learning to communicate with us, but that's no excuse or argument for the black man to repeat the same tragic mistake. . . . The whites need us, but we need the whites."

About the Authors

JOHN S. MORGAN is manager of employee publications for the General Electric Company in New York City, where he handles a wide variety of communications problems with emphasis on automation, training, and manpower planning. He has written a number of brochures on these subjects for General Electric, as well as a booklet, containing interviews with 50 Negroes employed by the company, designed to help show young Negroes the need for education and training.

A graduate of Yale University, Mr. Morgan was formerly on the editorial staff of *Steel Magazine,* where he wrote on labor and employee relations. He has also served on the advertising staff of White Motor Company.

Mr. Morgan is the author of *Getting Across to Employees,* a guide to effective communication on the job, and *Practical Guide to Conference Leadership* (McGraw-Hill Book Company); *Managing the Young Adults* and *Improving Your Creativity on the Job* (AMA); and *Business Faces the Urban Crisis* (Gulf Publishing Company).

RICHARD L. VAN DYKE is a special applications consultant in the Data Services Division of ITT and is at present on assignment in Latin America. A graduate of New York University in electrical engineering, he also served as metropolitan coordinator of the Plans for Progress Task Force on Youth Motivation in New York and as a committee member of both the Council of Concerned Black Executives, Inc. and the New York chapter of the National Association of Market Developers. Mr. Van Dyke's previous positions with the Service Bureau Corporation, a subsidiary of IBM, have been as engineering consultant on computer applications, as staff assistant to the director of personnel responsible for manpower planning and for implementing equal opportunity programs, and as a manager in contract programming.

Mr. Van Dyke also serves on the boards of directors of Van Dyke Products, Inc. and Achievement Consultants.